Welcome To The Millionaire Club !!

100 Business Lesson I learnt So Far To Become A Multi-Millionaire. And This Book Gonna Make You Rich Right here!!

This book is dedicated to my brother and my staff members who always helped me in thin and thick.

Introduction

Welcome to the smartest decision you've ever made by purchasing this book.

If you're sitting there wondering, let me tell you—this is absolutely going to be worth it. Buckle up, because this is the first time, besides the Alpha Male book, that I'm going to lay down all of my knowledge in the world about a particular subject. While Alpha Male was about masculinity, this book is about business—everything I know about making money.

So, how did this come about? I was convincing yet another person not to mix money with traditional university. I've done this many times. And while I'm not sure if I've always convinced them, I can confidently say that one of the biggest mistakes people make in life is relying solely on traditional education.

At some point, I thought, "Why not launch my own book and give people a genuine alternative to mainstream education?" I don't know about you, but personally, all I ever wanted to do was get rich. I didn't care if I got rich breaking rocks or being a professional fighter. I just wanted money.

I was not passionate about any particular business—I was passionate about money, and money only. So, if you've bought this book to learn how to run a business and get rich, congratulations! You're about to learn a whole lot, because I've run a variety of companies. Throughout this book, you'll discover the insights I've gained during my business career.

This is no-nonsense, no-fluff, and undoubtedly the hardest-hitting book ever written by a multi-millionaire on how to make money. Why? Because all the other multi-millionaires are lying to you. They're talking nonsense. We're cutting through the garbage and getting down to it with 100 business lessons I've learned across my career.

As I said, if you've made the decision to read this book, congratulations! Your worldview is about to change forever. I don't have a seatbelt on my chair, but if you do, put it on. If not, hold on tight—because we're about to get rich right here.

Lesson One: Speed

I tell this to everyone all the time, and nobody seems to understand what I'm trying to say, so I'm going to articulate it as clearly as I can: Speed is extremely important in business.

Everything that needs to be done must be done fast. That doesn't mean it has to be done cheaply or poorly—it means it has to be done quickly. People often confuse speed with a lack of quality. They think that if you do something quickly, it must be terrible. That's not the case.

When you're a professional fighter, your instructor pushes you to punch faster—"Faster! Faster!"—but you don't start punching like an idiot. You maintain the same quality of punch, just faster. No one in the modern world seems to get this. I want everything done now because speed is super important for a business, and I'm going to tell you why. Whatever you're thinking of doing, whatever business you're thinking of running, you need to do things quickly. Let me give you an example. Everyone knows how airplanes work: when a plane is flying through the sky, even if its engines fail, it won't instantly crash. It will continue to fly for a while because of its forward momentum. The wings are still creating lift as long as the plane is moving forward.

A business works exactly the same way. The key to business is to always be moving forward, always producing content, always doing everything as quickly as possible—while maintaining quality. Don't confuse speed with poor quality. You can do both at the same time.

If you have an idea right now and need a new website, don't let someone tell you it's going to take two weeks. No! It's going to take three days, and if that person can't do it, find someone who can. People have unrealistic, ridiculous time frames. They think things take forever, but they don't. Things can be done quickly.

 I know because I've done it. I've either pushed people to work faster or done things myself and seen how quickly things can actually get done. You know what I could do in two weeks? I could learn web design from scratch and build a website. And I know nothing about web design! So how is it that someone who does know web design needs two weeks to build one? It's garbage. Everyone is slow, and being slow is deadly for a company for two reasons.

Reason one: The faster you get things online, the faster you start making money. If you rush and get your website online today, and you make money today, that's one universe. But in another universe, it takes you a week to get online, and that week of potential income is lost forever. The longer it takes to get something done, the less money you'll make in total.

Reason two: Even if your company is already online, speed is still crucial. Take, for example, producing an ad. The faster you produce an ad, the faster it's out there, and the faster you get results. If you're fast enough, you could produce two ads in the time it takes others to produce one. Now you have double the advertising, and you're ahead of the game.

You have to attack, and you have to move quickly. People come to me all the time with business ideas. A week later, I ask them how things are going. They say, "What business?" They had an idea a week ago, but they haven't done anything yet. People are lazy, slow, and complacent—including you. Everything needs to happen instantly. Quickly. Fast. Speed. Attack.

I can't emphasize this enough. Lesson one: speed is everything. Nothing can be slow. There's no waiting until next Wednesday for a meeting. No, it's happening tomorrow. If they can't come to us until next week, we'll go to them tomorrow. We need to close the deal now. It's always about money, money, money, money—now. Speed is my entire business philosophy. If I had to give you just one important lesson, this would be it. That's why it's the first point. Everybody is slow. Once you start working like I do, you'll realize how slow everyone else is. And that's okay, but you must make things happen quickly. It's extremely important.

Lesson Two: Most of You Don't Know What a Business Is

Most of you don't even know what a business is. A business is money in. That's it. It's not about money out, it's not about your accountant, it's not about your logo, it's not about your website. A business is money flowing into your bank account.

A shopkeeper with cash in his pocket is a businessman, way more than some guy with a fancy logo and an accountant who's not getting paid. If you're getting paid, you own a business. Understand this, because it's crucial. This is the hustler's book, and hustlers understand how to make money.

Let me give you an example. People say, "I want to start a makeup company." And what do they do? They think, "Okay, I need to find some makeup, get a logo, register a trademark, and start ordering stock." They're already thinking about spending money. But as a businessman, your only focus is making money.

Here's the mistake: They're obsessed with spending,

not earning. "I need to find a makeup brand, test it out, get a logo, create labels, find a warehouse, build a website..." Where's the money in all that? This isn't a business, it's a spending spree.

Hustlers focus on making money, not spending it. Money coming in is the business, not money going out. So many people think they have a business, and they'll say, "Oh, I have this, and I have a registered trademark, and I own this..." They're stuck on paperwork and branding, but they're not making money. None of that matters if you're not getting paid. It's not a business until people are paying you.

You're better off having money coming in first, then spending. I can't emphasize this enough. It's much better to have money in the bank and then spend it, than the other way around.

If I were starting a makeup brand, I wouldn't waste time with all that nonsense. I'd build a website, put up some makeup with prices, and start advertising. Bang! Now I'm making money. I'm getting orders. I don't have any makeup, I don't have a warehouse, I don't have a logo. I don't even have a trademark, but I'm making money. With money, you can fix problems. Once I have cash in the bank, I'll email everyone who ordered and say, "The product you're interested in is in high demand, so there's a slight delay in delivery. But don't worry, we'll throw in a free gift for your patience. Thank you for being a valued customer!" Now, people are waiting. They're happy with the free gift, and they'll be patient. Now, you have three or four weeks to find the makeup, get it shipped, and get the orders out. But you've got the money. You didn't have to spend a dime before making a dime. You've got cash coming in, now you just need to fulfill the orders. And that brings us back to lesson number one: speed.

Find the makeup, slap on a logo, and get it out the door. It makes more sense than spending first without any money coming in. Imagine if you spend all your money, try to advertise, and no one buys? You've lost. My way, I advertise, no one buys, no big deal. Who cares? It's not like I've got 500 boxes of makeup sitting in my bedroom. A business is money in. When you want to start a business, your only concern is how to get money in.

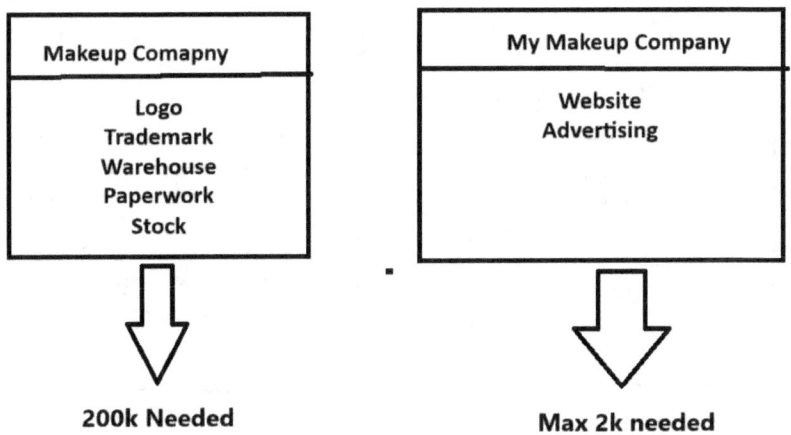

Everyone else starts talking about offices, laptops, and hiring staff. Why do you need an office if no one's paid you yet? Why do you need a new laptop when you haven't made any money? You don't need anything until people start giving you money. Money in is a business. Money out is vanity.

It's easy for me to think, "I'll buy an office, buy laptops, hire staff, get an accountant, sort out the tax records, register the company online, get business cards, get a logo, and get it trademarked." But I'm just spending money and wasting time. Nobody's paying me, so it's not a business. When someone comes to me with a business plan, my first question is, "Where's the money?" When you want to start a business, the first question is, "Where's the money?"

How are you going to get paid? PayPal? Stripe? Bitcoin? How will people pay you? How will you convince them to pay you?

Makeup Comapny	My Makeup Company
If no one buys lost 200k	If no one buys I lost almost nothing or lil amount

Once you figure that out, you can work out the rest. A business is money in, nothing else. That's lesson number two. And it's crucial, because it will save you from a lot of failures in the future. And that leads us to idea number three...

Lesson Three: Start Cheap, Start Now

Alright, listen up, because this is a game-changer. Lesson number three, and it's a big one. I've already touched on it in lesson two, but this needs its own spotlight.

People come to me all the time with business ideas. They think they need some big investment. Maybe they're developing an app, and they need a little cash for development, fair enough. But then there's the rest, asking for crazy amounts of money – 50 grand, 100 grand, 200 grand! "I need this much to start my business!"

Look, you can start a business on a shoestring if you play your cards right. Let's go back to our beautiful example, our makeup company. The traditional way, you're talking about needing at least 200 grand. You need an office, logos, trademarks, stock, staff, company incorporation, taxes, accountants, advertising budgets... you name it, it costs money. But here's the hustler's way: You build a website, throw up some pictures, pretend you've got a whole bunch of inventory (you don't), and start taking orders. You can launch this whole thing for five grand. That's five grand for the website, a 195 grand difference. Now, the problem is you'll start getting money in without any products to ship, right? But remember lesson number one, speed? You're a hustler, you're quick, you're industrious, you find a way to get those orders filled.

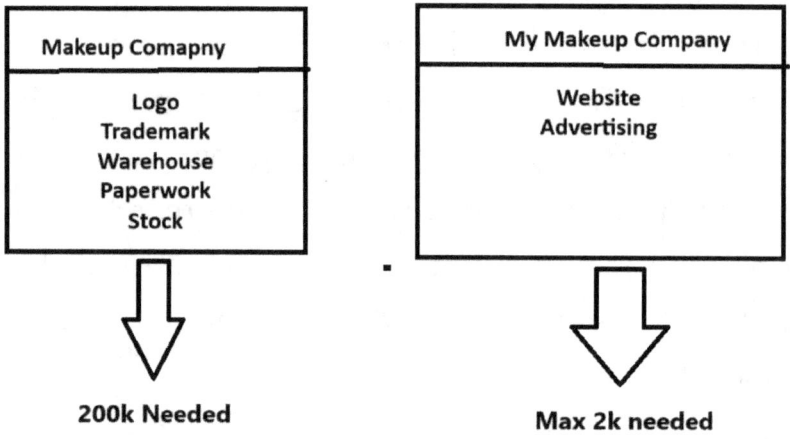

Worst case, you refund them. But at least you've tested the market. You've figured out if your idea has legs. And, let's be honest, both companies might fail, right? But with the traditional model, you're down 200 grand. My way? Five grand.

Makeup Comapny	My Makeup Company
If no one buys lost 200k	If no one buys I lost almost nothing or lil amount

Why risk a fortune when you can start small? And for the same price, you could launch 40 businesses. One of them will hit, because at five grand a pop, you can afford to experiment. Get this into your head, starting a business doesn't need to be expensive. I'm a millionaire, a multi-millionaire, and I don't spend more than five grand on a launch. Five grand, max. If I see money coming in, then maybe I'll invest more.

You can build a company off the money you're making, and you never need to spend your own money. That's how you launch a company. Now, some people will say, "But what about this, what about that?" Look, if you're trying to build a plane company to compete with Boeing, yeah, you'll need a lot of cash. But this book is for you guys out there looking to make money, start a business, or grow your existing small company.

One of the biggest mistakes you can make is investing a ton of money when you're broke. You don't have anything to lose. But when you're rich, it's easy to make mistakes because you have a lot of money to lose.

Start cheap, for free. Focus on money coming in, and hold off on all the fancy stuff until you've got a cash flow. That way, you can start lots of companies, you've got money rolling in, and you can reinvest that money to build your business.

Makeup Comapny	My Makeup Company
Don't focus on cashflow. Focus on Money out Its vanity	Focus on Cashflow. Focus on Money in than spending. Its a business

Every company I've ever built has been done this way. When I got my first deal for my company, I had a Blackberry, a business card, and I went to their office and signed the deal. I had a free business bank account, no tax incorporation, nothing. They paid me, and I used that money to buy an office. Done. I started an agency like this. I bought a laptop, a Blackberry, got some business cards, landed my first deal, and built my whole business off the money coming in.

If you can do it with an agency, you can do it with almost anything. This is advertising back in the day, before the internet was huge. Everyone wanted to advertise cheaply. You start a company with a Blackberry, that's how it works. This approach lets you start more businesses, see what's viable, what's going to make money, without the risk.

This is how you approach businesses, not like some weak-willed loser. Lesson number three, get it in your head: Money in, start cheap, go for speed, and don't let some fancy-pants business guru tell you otherwise.

These first three lessons – speed, money in, and starting cheap – they're more valuable than anything you'll learn from some overpriced business course. If you do this, you'll be amazed at how hard it is to fail, how hard it is to lose money. And you can start practically any company you want.

You stick to these three rules, and you'll launch companies for next to nothing. Nothing can go wrong, you're unstoppable.

Now get out there and dominate.

Lesson Four: Family and Friends Are, Your Best Staff

Alright, here's lesson four, and it's going to ruffle some feathers. But listen up, because this is how you build an empire.

People say, "Don't mix business with family. Don't mix business with friends." That's a load of crap. The reason they say that is because they're too dumb to get along with anyone long enough to make money.

I guarantee you have family members who can make you money. I guarantee you have an 18-year-old niece, nephew, cousin, brother, whoever, who knows more about computers than you do. There's a kid out there who knows more about Photoshop than you do, and they're probably bored and need a job. You can start a company right now. Call up your cousins, nieces, nephews, anyone 15 or 16 years old who's stuck in school, bored, and tell them you're starting a company. "I'm making you a director. You're going to get ten percent of the business. You're going to do everything I say. By the time you're 20, you're going to be rich."

Better staff as hustler
Family and friends. Young kids. College students. Broke boys

Not good staff
Age old person. already working people . Expensive persons.

I'm not saying exploit them, but use their skills. Start a business. You need young people, not some old geezer. Why? Because young people have nothing to lose. Hire a 30-year-old, and he's got rent and car payments. He can't afford to fail. But an 18-year-old? He just plays video games. If the business goes down, no big deal.

You must have friends or family who are young enough to have time to waste. Don't hire people who can't afford to not pay their rent. Hire people who live for free. If you've got friends with kids, go to them and say, "Your kid is 15 and good with computers? I'm starting a company, let him work with me for free, see how it goes." They'll love it! Their kid is getting real-world experience. "Yeah, good idea. What's the business name?" Boom! There are free workers everywhere. And if they're not free, they're cheap, and they're everywhere. You just need to use them.

 Let's say you're starting a website business, right? You don't know anything about building websites. You find an 18-year-old and tell him to learn. You convince him it's a good idea. Then you start taking orders. You become the middleman. The 18-year-old works for free. You can do websites cheap. I'll do a whole website for 300 bucks: half upfront, half when it's done. People love that! "300 for a website? Yeah, I'm in!" You take the 150 bucks, give 50 to the 18-year-old, and tell him he gets another 50 when he's done. He gets 100 bucks, you get 200, and you didn't do anything.

 The best staff you can find are young people, and in most cases, they know more than the old geezers anyway. Especially about technology. Young people are fantastic. I love hiring 18 or 19-year-old kids. They know more than me about TikTok, Instagram, all that stuff. I'm 30, I'm not even old. These kids are telling me what to do, and I'm like, "Go! How long will it take?" "A week." I say, "No, I need it tomorrow. Show me tomorrow." Speed, back to lesson one!

You already have workers for your business. You just don't use them because you're lazy. Contact them right now. Get started!

Lesson Five: Command physical Respect

Alright, lesson five, and this one's going to make some people uncomfortable. But I'm not here to coddle you, I'm here to make you rich.

I'm not going to waste your time with the fluff all the other "business gurus" preach. They talk about positive thinking and all that nonsense. Easy for them to say when they're already rich and have no real business skills.

But this? This is the real deal. Command respect.

Here's an example: I still talk to one of my friends sometimes. He's a good guy, good heart, but he just loves smoking. I'm good at business because I command respect. And I command respect because I'm a physical specimen of a man. It's reality. I look like a professional fighter.

Whether I'm running my company or pitching for my advertising agency, there's a level of respect humans have for other humans who are physically strong. My friend is a big black guy. The way he acts, the way he treated his staff, he could get away with things. He couldn't get away with that if he was an obese white guy.

It's evolutionary. Humans respect people who are viewed as strong. They trust them. If you want to run a business and get people to spend money with you, the best thing you can do is hit the gym. Get in shape. People will see, "Okay, he's obviously not afraid of hard work, he's disciplined." There are things that are spoken without being spoken, and having a physical presence is one of them. It helps in every aspect of business.

When I was selling advertising, I'd stand up in front of people and say, "I guarantee you, your spending will be worth it with me. I guarantee you'll get double back when you see your products." When I said that, as a big strong guy, who they could tell had trained hard, was disciplined, wasn't afraid of hard work, it was more valuable than if I was a fat piece of shit. It's just going to work.

Go to the gym. Command a physical presence. I'm not saying beat people up, I'm saying when you have a physical presence, your words have more weight. It helps with everything.

Everything I know about running an agency, I learned a lot about business. I started cheap, with a laptop I already had, and a service. I figured out how to get money in before I figured out how to produce the videos. People were sending me money for these feature-length videos that I couldn't even make yet. I didn't even have a camera. But it was all about speed. Get everything produced quickly.

I did all the same things with all my businesses, but the reason I had so many clients, listen to me, is because I'm me. I'm big and strong. If you want to run your business, don't neglect physical presence.

Now, you can be successful without it. There are plenty of successful people who aren't big and strong. But I'm talking about what I know, what I've learned. And what I'm saying is, it will help you. Even if you're Bill Gates, and he was super successful, he would have been even more successful if he was a big strong dude.

It's never going to hurt you to be bigger and stronger in life, whether it's business or anything else. Commanding a physical presence will always help you. It shows discipline. It shows you understand hard work. It makes your word more valuable. Sometimes in business, all you have is your word. You have to promise people, and they have to believe you. If you're a big strong dude, people just believe you more.

This is the book for you. I told you, there's no nonsense, no garbage. If you want to run a company, start going to the gym. Get big, get strong. It's going to help you make money sooner or later, I guarantee it. This is point five, don't neglect it. It's true.

Even if it only helps you ten percent, that's a lot. Ten percent is the difference between success and failure. Ten percent is the difference between a little bit of money and a lot of money. Ten percent is huge. If you're selling a million-dollar product and you have a 20% margin, that's 200 grand. If you have an extra ten percent margin because you're the big strong guy, that's 300 grand. Bang! That's an extra 100 grand a year. That's a 911, that's a Porsche. It's a big difference.

Don't neglect number five, because it's real. The closer you are to good physical condition, the more likely you are to be respected. The more likely you are to say things and people believe you. Get in physical shape. That's point five. Commanding respect is always going to help you throughout life, especially in business.

Lesson Six: Resell to Your Existing Customers

Alright, here's the lowdown on how to make the easiest money you'll ever see.

When my advertising agency was struggling, we were selling these $18,000- $19,000 deals. We survived so long because we knew to resell to the people we'd already sold to.

We'd get people to sign up, pay the money, make their ad, show them the ad, and hope they liked it. If they did, we'd try to sell them a "bonus package." We'd say, "We've got this huge purchase coming up from a big company, and we're getting it extremely cheap. For an extra five grand, we can run another ad campaign for you." Some garbage like that. We'd try to sell them this extra package because it had some profit for us.

If they said no, we'd basically done all the work for nothing. But if they said yes, we'd make a profit. We'd sell it for five grand, and it was like four grand in profit. That's how we were surviving. If we tried to sell them the bigger packages upfront, they wouldn't buy. But if we sold them the smaller package and then tried to upsell them later, we had a 60-70% upsell rate if they liked their ad.

The easiest money you'll ever make is selling to people who've already bought from you before, as long as you did a decent job. We did it after they saw their ad. We never tried to sell them before they saw the ad because it was much harder.

If you do a good job, or even a halfway decent job, the best customers you're going to have are the ones who've already bought from you. You should already know this about business. It's easy. It's so much easier to sell to someone who's already bought from you than to sell to someone new.

A lot of you reading this might have already bought something from me. Congratulations, you must know a lot of things. But this is important, this is true.

I get people with different businesses calling me for advice all the time. Two months ago, this guy called me up saying he was struggling for cash. He asked me to borrow money. I said, "I won't tell you who he is or what his business is, but you'll know. Some of you will know." I said, "Okay, how much do you need?" He said, "200 grand." I said, "How many customers do you have? We all know how many customers are on your database."

He said, "About 10,000." I said, "Bro, there's your 200 grand! Put together an email campaign, do a huge discount, let them pay full price. These people have bought from you before. Put it all together and blast it out there. There's your 200 grand. What do you need me for? These people have bought from you before, and you delivered. Your money is sitting right there, go get it!"

So easy to sell to people who've already bought from you before. If you've done a half-decent job in business, you don't need to sell to a ton of people. If you can sell to the same people over and over again, you're golden. It's much easier to sell to the same people than to keep finding new ones. Keep that in mind, especially during times when you need cash or you're trying to raise cash or increase cash flow.

If you have a company, you're making a bit of money, and you're thinking, "I want to make more, what can I do?" Don't look at advertising more. Don't look at getting new customers. Don't look at a new product launch. The first thing you should do is resell to people who've already bought from you.

That's the easiest money you'll ever make. Don't forget that. You're going to need to be able to pull that ace out of your sleeve at certain points in your business career. You'll need to be able to generate money from thin air. Keep that in mind. That's point six.

Lesson Seven: Don't Get Legal Until You Get Rich

Alright, listen up, because this one is HUGE. This is the kind of advice that separates the hustlers from the wannabes.

We're talking hustling here. I'm giving you the hacks to becoming rich. Don't get legal before you're rich. You can fix your legal shit when you've already made money.

It's like what we were talking about earlier. I know so many people who have registered a company, registered for VAT, registered with the tax man, have an accountant, and they haven't made a dime yet.

I'll make a million dollars in most of my companies before I even consider messing around with tax forms, talking to an accountant, or registering any companies. It's all secondary. Until you've proven the viability of your company, until you've got money coming in, don't worry about all that.

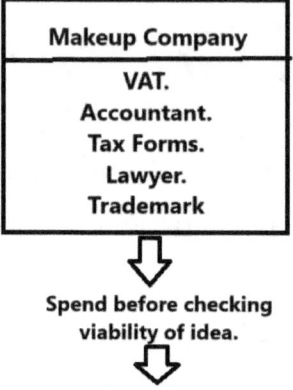 

When you're rich and have money in the bank, then worry about that stuff. Don't waste your time, energy, and money doing all that legal crap before you even know if your business is going to work. Don't do it. It's counterproductive, it's expensive, and it's a time sink.

If every time I had to start a company or an idea I had to go register it, get an accountant, do tax forms, do VAT forms, what a waste of time. I've started maybe 100 companies in my life, and 20 of them made money. That means 80 times I would've had to go through all that for failed businesses. Don't do that.

I know so many people who have a company legally,

but they don't have a company in reality. It exists as a legal entity, but it doesn't provide cash. A company provides cash. If you're a street shopkeeper, you own a company, much more than the guy with all the legal entities who isn't making money.

We're hustlers here, this is the hustler's book. We're not interested in costs until we've seen the money in. Don't get legal before you get rich. You don't need any legal shit. You need a website, a domain name, and that's it. You don't need any legal things before you get rich. Don't make that mistake.

The reason people do that is because it makes them feel better. They feel like they have a company. People say, "I want to start a company." They don't know what to do, they don't know how to make money. They think, "Well, if I spend money and set it all up legally, then I've got a company." They feel better inside, like they've achieved something. But they haven't achieved anything because they're still not making money. Don't fall into these traps.

You can walk around telling everyone you have a company because you spent money. Anyone can spend money. Making money is hard, spending money is easy. Don't do that. Vanity. "I own a company on paper." Garbage. Get all that off your plate until money's coming in the bank. Don't get legal before you get rich. Extremely important.

Lesson eight: Family and brotherhood

Hustle with your family members. Brotherhood is important and pool up the money even when you are working in job or hustling or even when you are rich,it will always help you to live better.Collectively own everything.

Listen, everyone's got people who are so valuable to them that they wouldn't stab them in the back for a billion dollars and a thousand women. Those are the people you want to work with. As long as you're sure they share your sentiments, pool your resources. Live in the same house if you're broke. If you're both working dead-end jobs, rent one room together if you have to. If you're good friends, and you meet a woman, tell her to take a walk for an hour and come back. That's one of the keys to my success.

Lesson nine: Use What You Got

Alright, this is lesson nine and it's all about resourcefulness. You're gonna hear this a lot, because it's a game-changer.

This ties into lessons two and three. I just gave you the example of your 18-year-old cousin who can make websites. Now you've got a website company, or your 18-year-old cousin who can do, I don't know... whatever. Congratulations, use what you got.

I made a lot of money with my agency, millions and millions of dollars. I came up with that idea by sticking to this principle: Use what you got.

Right now, if you're sitting there, make a list of everything you have. I mean everything. You have a house? Write it down, even if it's rented. You have a car? Write it down, even if it's leased. You have physical strength? Write it down, even if you're just a strong guy.

When I was making my list, I wrote everything down: "I've got skills in business and video editing." Okay, how can those skills make me money? "Television advertising."

But that takes a lot of money to set up. Remember costs? How do I make money? So I looked at the costs for TV advertising, and I realized it's too expensive. It's too big of a risk. I could lose 300, 400 grand. Can't risk that. How can I get money in? How can I get money in for having adverts without spending money out?

My first idea was television, but then I looked at the costs. Okay, so how do people spend money on TV ads, especially to sell more and promote their brand? How can I do that without going into the TV industry? Well, the internet! If I put them on the internet, it's cheap. This is literally how I thought. I stuck to my business principles. Okay, it's cheap, start looking, I discovered websites. Alright, I've got the skills, I've got a laptop, I've got the internet. Boom! The day I had the idea, the same day I was making money. Remember rule number one? I didn't spend any money, but I was making money because I refused to allow myself to spend.

Then I started making money with the agency because I knew I had the internet, I knew I had laptops, I knew I had the skills. Use what you got. Look around. Use what you have, make a long list, and you'll start thinking of business ideas, and they're going to come to you like the online ad agency came to me.

But then you're going to sit there and say, "Okay, this is a good idea, but I can't afford that." But then you're going to go back to the other lessons I've taught you. Okay, this is how much it would cost to set it up that way, but how can I get the money in that this would generate without all the costs?

If you do that, sit there with a piece of paper, write everything down, and stick to the principles I've taught you so far about how to start businesses, you might find a business you can start for a couple grand. You've already got your staff, a couple grand, you've got an idea, you try it, it doesn't work, you lost a couple grand. It does work, boom! You're rich. That simple. If it starts to work, speed, speed, speed, speed, more, more, more!. It's really not that complicated.

This is how hustlers get rich. It's really, really simple. So use what you got. A lot of you already have things you can use, you just don't use them. Just for example, Uber. I know Uber doesn't pay a lot. But you know what everyone loves to do when they first get their driving license? Drive.

Maybe you have a 19- or 20-year-old cousin or some people who need a job. He just learned to drive, get him on Uber. Rent a car, find a way to rent a car with unlimited mileage per month. Tell him he's going to do 10 hours of Uber a day. You can track it in the Uber app to make sure he's not breaking the speed limit, so he drives safe. Put him on Uber, pay for his gas, give him half the money, keep half for yourself. Boom! Done! Set him up, get him ready. I didn't plan it, I'm just telling you because this is how I think as a hustler. I don't need to sit and think, I just know there's money, and I find a way to get it. That's how I am.

So right now, you've got cousins out there who aren't driving Uber. If you can convince them to drive Uber, well then... there's money happening. You're just not doing anything. Look around, make a full list of what you have, stick to the business principles, and find a way to get money in without spending money out. You won't lose. That's what I did with the agency, and it made me millions of dollars. Millions.

I ended up with huge numbers of clients, all because one client and one website. I started with one client, made money, bought another laptop, got another laptop, got another staff member. Two clients, made money, bought a bigger apartment. Three clients, four, five... bang, bang, bang, bang! Before you know it, I had an empire because I stuck to my business principles. I never spent money I didn't make first. I never spent a dollar out of my pocket that I hadn't already made first from the company. I started that from zero, just like I started my advertising agency from zero.

This is why, when people come to me and say, "I want to start a business, I need an investment," I sit there and think, "You don't know about business." Because if you knew about business and your idea was really good, you wouldn't need my money. You'd pull it off for zero. If you're talented and your idea is good, you don't need money. If you can't make it work for zero or for very little, then it probably wouldn't work anyway, and you'd just lose a whole bunch of money.

Because if it's a good idea and it will work, then money will start coming in fast, and you'll have the money you need. If no one's sending you money to give you the money you need, then the idea doesn't work anyway.

Lesson ten: Staff Must Make Money or Save Time

Alright, let's talk about staff. This is a big one, and it's gonna make you think differently about who you hire and how you manage them.

I know a lot of people starting companies or wanting to start businesses, and the first thing they say is, "I need an assistant." "I need this staff member." "I need that staff member."

Staff need a clear objective. Here's the simple, magical rule for staff: Staff either make you money or save you time, or you don't need them.

A salesperson, sales staff, they sell things, they bring money in. You'll be able to see exactly how much money that staff member made you each week. You'll be able to make sure that they made you more than they cost you. Fine.

Other staff members are going to save you time. Even if it's a general assistant or a PA, you'll be able to see the time saved with the tasks they've completed. You need to sit down with a piece of paper, once a month, once every couple of weeks, whatever, and audit your staff.

Staff Member: How much money do they make? How much do they cost? Positive or negative?

Staff Member: What tasks did they complete? How much longer would it take me to do those tasks? Is it worth the money?

Because if you could have done those tasks in your free time while you were watching TV, then you don't need that staff member. Fire them and save the cash.

You have to audit your staff very specifically by this method. They either save you time, they make you money, or you don't need them.

Anyone who's worked any kind of job knows, if you go into any company, most people are doing nothing. I've worked so many jobs, and everyone did nothing. If you take out coffee breaks, cigarette breaks, chit-chatting in the office, most people do nothing. I'm very sure you could fire 50% of the people in nearly any company, and the company would be just fine if the other 50 did some real work. Everyone's lazy. Big companies are inefficient because they haven't got the time to do this. But you're not going to have a big company. You're a hustler. You're going to have a few staff members, you're going to make millions of dollars, and you're going to make sure they're either making you money or saving you time.

Now, if the amount of time they're saving you isn't enough or they're not making enough money to cover their wages, they gotta go. You gotta be ruthless in this game. This is the magic formula for staff.

When people say to me, "I want to start a company, I need an assistant," I say, "An assistant to do what? Oh, just to help me with things. What things? What things will they help with? How long do those things take? How much time is that going to save you? And why don't you have the time to do them yourself? Because you want to watch TV? Because you need to relax? Because you're afraid you'll burn out? Shut up, it's garbage. It's all garbage. You want to feel important and tell someone what to do. That's not how you get rich."

This is the magic staff formula: Do they make me money? Do they save me time? Write it all down, work it out, and if it's not good enough, they gotta go. Simple. That's how you manage staff. I get asked so many questions about staff. Make money, save me time, done.

Another thing that's important with staff is you have to teach them your business ethics. Whenever I've had a staff member, I've argued with them plenty of times because everything must be done quickly. That's how I work, that's how I want them to work.

I am 100% certain that even if it's only by one percent, the fact that I'm uncompromising about wanting things done quickly, things get done quickly or quicker. If I didn't say anything, it might take 10 seconds. If I complain, it might take nine seconds. It might take 10 seconds. If I complain, it might take nine seconds. It might only be a tiny saving, but that's how I work. That's how the people I work with, I want them to work. Speed is everything.

When you get new staff members on board, make sure they understand your business principles, especially number one, because that is your business mantra: Speed. If you have a salesman and he's selling and he's doing fantastic, that's good. You can sit him down and say, "You know what, you're doing a fantastic job, you're making lots of money, I'm very, very proud of you. Look, you're making this, this, this, this, you've done really well. But, you're hitting targets. Only one thing I want to talk about: How quickly you work."

"What do you mean? I'm hitting targets."

"Yeah, you are hitting targets, but when you're inputting information into the system, I think we can get that done quicker. There must be a faster way we can get that done." Free up his time. If he does things quicker, he has more free time to sell more products, he'll make more money. Speed! No one ever works fast enough. When I was learning karate, it's never quick enough. It has to be quicker, has to be quicker.

In fighting, there's no such thing as too quick. Everything must be faster, all the time. It's the same in your business. All the time. Faster, all of it, all the time.

If your assistant is saving you time, if they work faster, they save you more time because they have more time to do more things to save you time. Faster, all the time. So even if they're both performing, you still have to re-incentivize and re-illuminate point one. Point one is super, super important. If you do that, you're going to get more out of your staff, more money's going to be made, more work can get done, it's better for everyone as a whole.

I learned this in business. If it was menial work, more work happened in the same time frame, more work got done, that made me more valuable as a staff member. That's how people valued you as well as me. Always do something. You've got to be the same, right? That's the first 10 lessons. We have 90 more. The first 10 lessons of this book. I bet you're sitting there already and your mind's blown. You're sitting there like, "Whoa, I've learned so much, I didn't think of it that way."

Read it two or three times. These things need to

sink in like second nature to you. You need to be able to recite them one by one. We've talked about how you start companies, what you prioritize in a company, how you make sure everything's done quickly and why that's so important, how you manage staff, how you find ideas to relaunch companies, what staff members you can get.

Lesson Eleven: Outsource Cheaply

If there's something you can't do, and you need someone to do it, you need to outsource cheaply. Either find a student, like I said earlier about your niece and nephew, or find students. Students are fantastic because students need money. They need money to do projects, whatever. Let's say you need a video, find a film student. They'll do it cheaper than a film company. Find students, or use Fiverr. Outsource cheaply, and never, ever hire if you can avoid it. Please, don't hire another company to do your work.

 As a company, as a hustler, I'm not trying to teach you how to be a CEO. I'm teaching you how to make five or six million dollars a year, so you can buy supercars and enjoy your life as a hustler. You want to be here at the top. I'm the hustler, I'm the CEO, and underneath me, I want everyone... let's say I develop an app, I need an app development company, but if I can help it, I'll hire a student to make my app. Ideally, you want individuals below you, all people. Maybe you'll need a company below you to do something, so let's make this specific.

Let's say I have an app company. My relationship with the people, other staff members, is always going to be better and cheaper than my relationship with a company. Because a company isn't interested in making you rich. I know you think that people aren't interested either, but bear with me. A company is interested in making itself rich. They're very different things.

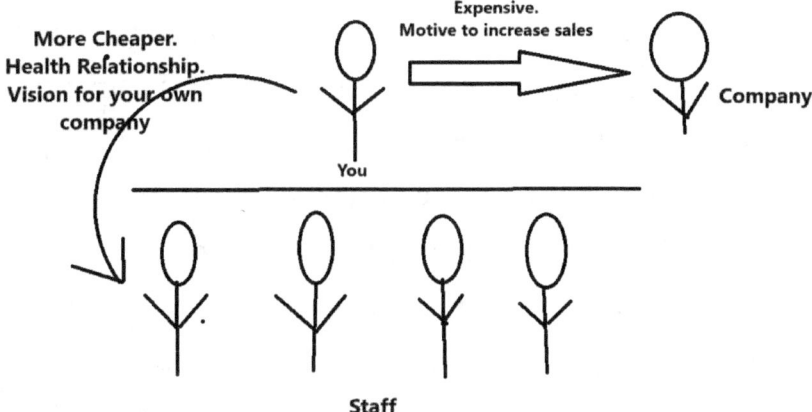

Let's take an example, a website. If I need a new website, and I tell a person who works for me to make that website, me and the person have a personal, vested interest in that website. I can discuss it with him personally, we can get it done.

If I hire a company to make my website, it gets added to their list of work. Then this company thinks, "How can we get more websites?" Do you understand where I'm coming from? The person who's tasked with the website has one job: Make my website. The company who's tasked with the website has two jobs: Make the website, and find more people who need websites, more customers. They need to do two things. And if they're smart (and some of them are), if they had to choose between delivering your website on time or taking on more work and clients and taking more money, they'll take the money. Their primary focus is not your site, their primary focus is generating money. Do you understand? There's a huge difference.

This person's primary focus is completing his job for his boss. This person's primary focus is not completing the job for the boss, it's getting more money from somewhere else. Has nothing to do with you. Fair enough, they may have more people in different departments, but that's still the primary goal of the individuals, the primary goal of the company. Plus, the company is more expensive.

You have to try to outsource cheaply. You want

to have individuals you work with. Now, if an individual has a company, fine, that's still an individual. When someone goes, "I'm me and I have my company," I see that as an individual. I don't see big companies as people I want to work with. If I want a website, I don't want to go into some office full of people making websites. I don't like that. I've never had a positive experience with that. It's always expensive. They always have other jobs and other things to do. Their primary goal is making money. They don't really give a shit about you.

Now, if you need something very specific and personalized, and you need a really big company, okay, do it. But in most cases, you don't. Try to work with people, try to outsource cheaply, try to use students. This is number 11. Nearly anything you need done, a student can do. You can find students, and students are, drumroll, broke, which means they work cheap. Find students! If you don't know how to do something, find a student. Try to avoid going to companies. Companies have a different objective than keeping you happy.

If you have good staff under you, you become like a team, you become like family. Everyone wants to work together, everyone wants everything to work. If you're a good leader, your staff genuinely want everything to work, and you genuinely want your staff to be happy. It's a happy medium. Everyone wants success. The company doesn't really give a shit if your company fails. If you've paid the invoice, they don't give a shit. You paid the invoice, they have to deliver a website, whatever. They've got 10 other people to make websites for. Oh, your company failed? Big whoop!

Work with people with vested interests, students, young people, try to outsource cheap, try to avoid hiring another company to do anything. As a hustler, you want to have you at the top, individuals you can trust below you. That is the happiest company structure. You don't want to be working with lots of companies. I know guys who are trying to start businesses, they hire a website company, they hire an accountancy firm, they hire this, they hire that. I'm like, "All it is is you at the top, company below you, company below you, company below you, all trying to send you invoices and add you to their list of past customers." Don't do that. You won't get rich very quickly doing that. Trust me.

Lesson Twelve: If You Don't Spend Money, It's Hard to Fail

This is key. It's very hard to fail if you don't spend money. Now, if you have a successful business and you're sitting on a ton of cash, and you don't upgrade your business and then you go out of business, that's a shit move, obviously. You should have spent money. Yeah, if you're Blockbuster and you're sitting there waiting for people to rent videos, and you didn't invest in a streaming service like Netflix, and your business went under, yeah, you failed up. You should have spent money.

But at the beginning of a company, as a hustler, if you don't spend money, it's very hard to fail. 99% of business ruins are, "I spent cash, and I can't get it back. I spent cash, and I lost it. I spent cash, and now I don't have enough cash."

If you don't spend it, it's very difficult to fail. And that's why being broke is so liberating. I was happier starting businesses when I was broke.

If you're watching this and you're broke and you're living at home with your mom, you are lucky. If everything goes wrong, you still have somewhere to sleep, you're still going to eat, you don't have to worry about a mortgage payment, you don't have to worry about a car payment. If everything fails, you're still okay.

If you're in a position where you're semi-successful, you have a BMW and an apartment, now you can't afford to fail. You're going to lose everything. This is the point. Spending money is the easiest way to go wrong. If you don't blow money, it's very hard to fail.

And that's why we go back to the way I teach you to start businesses, for nearly free. Don't spend money. If you're going to spend money, spend it on knowledge, information. This book is gonna save you thousands, hundreds of thousands of dollars. But in general, I see people, and they're so happy to spend money. Don't spend your money because it's very hard to fail then.

If you're not spending money, if you've got a hustle, it doesn't matter what it is, and it's bringing money in, yeah, and you're not spending money all the time, you'll be okay. Now, I'm not saying be tight, I'm not

not saying be stingy, I'm not saying any of that. I'm saying be careful, and think, "Do I need to spend this money right now?"

When you have to decide if you're going to spend money or not, the question is, "Is it going to make me more money?"

Let's take our makeup brand. You have your makeup brand. I chose makeup because I don't know anything about makeup. I'm a man. It's just a general thing. You have your makeup brand, you have your website, you're doing some advertising, you've got a few makeup YouTubers using your products, and you're doing some advertising, you're bringing in money, right? You're bringing money in right now. You're all working from home. You're from home. You've got boxes around your bedroom, you're working on a laptop, you're making money.

Now you have some money you can spend. How do you spend that money? I'm asking you, I already know the answer. The answer is you spend the money in a way that will bring more money in. Let's say you're semi-successful now. You might sit there and think, "Well, I want an office now, I need to get an office." No, you want an office. You don't need an office. You're making money without an office. Setting up an office, is that going to bring in more orders? How is being in an office when your website is exactly the same going to bring in more orders? It's not. It's not going to change anything.

If you spend that money on more YouTubers talking about your products, you'll bring in more money. Only spend money if it's going to directly, if you can see the clear path to how it's going to lead to more money in. Or don't spend it. Too many people get ruined because they just go, "Oh yeah, let me invest in..." Oh, I need an office. Or, "We need to..." I get approached with this all the time. "You need a backend." "You need to spend money." I'll go, "It's only a few months ago, fifteen thousand euro, he wanted to build me this super backend because I have tech that's all run on Telegram and all these bots. So when someone buys a product, it automatically links to their Telegram ID, automatically adds them in and out of the website, checks what other products they have, links them...". I'm sitting there going, "Okay, I see how that would be useful, a huge, very complicated technical backend, but I don't see how that's going to bring more people in the front. I'm a millionaire, he wants 15 grand, which is nothing. I don't see how me having all this fancy shit behind my website at this current stage, maybe at a later date, is going to make more people buy from my website. But why do I need it? All I need is people to buy. I don't need this backend, this big, huge backend for money that may speed things up once they've already purchased. But right now, I'm doing everything manually with staff, and the staff are competent, and it's getting done. It's fine. So why do I need to spend this money? It goes against my business principles."

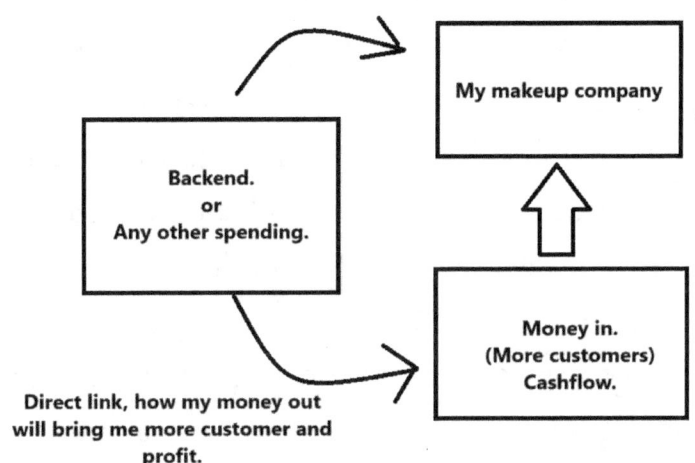

When someone explains to me how this backend will convince more people at the front end to buy, then I'll be interested. But until then, if I'm going to spend 15 grand, I'm going to spend it on bringing more people in the front door. Now, if I get overloaded, and there's no possible way I can deliver on my products, I'll buy the backend. But until that happens, I'm only interested in one thing: money in.

What are the other lessons I taught you in the first two, the first 10 lessons? One of the lessons was, "What's a business?" A business is money in. This is a business. Money in is your focus. As long as you have this, you will be okay. My agency succeeded for a year, and it would have been for many years because of this. As long as you have money in, nothing will go wrong. If this goes, you're done, over. You can have the best website, the best cash reserves, and the best backend in the world. If no one's ordering, you're going to go out of business.

If you have lots of orders, no cash reserves, and no backend, but people are buying and buying and buying, you've got a business. This is it. This is your focus. If you're going to spend money, it has to directly lead to this.

Don't fall for the geek shit, especially with websites. I've had so many people come at me and go, "Oh, and it's going to be a program, programming, and very interesting..." I understand why that sounds like something I need, but I don't see how it's going to convince more people to buy from me. People buy from me because I'm me, and I give value. That's why they buy. And manually, I make sure everyone ends up where they need to be, and it's fine.

You could argue that this might speed things up, and that's going to go back to number one, speed. This is going to speed things up, giving my staff more time. But I already do my staff time equation, remember, staff time saving. I'm very happy with the amount of time that's being saved, and the money each staff member's making me. I have a good equation right now for my staff. It doesn't need adjusting. My staff are all fantastic.

So I don't need to invest a bunch of money. If you're going to spend money, be careful, and if you're going to spend money, you need to see a clear link to how it's going to bring more money in. This is your business. Nothing else is your business. The rest is shit.

Lesson Thirteen: Businesses Won't Last Forever

Alright, listen up, because this is a lesson that cost me a lot. I'm letting you in on the biggest mistake I made with my first agency.

You think your business is going to last forever? It won't. And if a business won't last forever, you need to get rich quick, and you need to put yourself before your business.

The biggest mistake I made with my agency is that I was so desperate to keep it afloat. I wasn't taking any of my own money. I bought a new car, I gave myself a little bit of money, but if I could go back in time, I would have milked that cow. I had money in the bank, but to keep it surviving, I didn't want to take so much money. I reduced the amount of wages we were taking. Kept it low. So when it all blew up, I wasn't sitting on any money. I kept the company alive at the expense of me. If I could go back in time, by the time it all blew up, I'd be sitting on half a million.

Look after yourself first. And this is very, very important, because no business lasts forever. Doesn't matter what the business is. Even my advertising business, which worked years ago, would never work today. Calling people on the phone, trying to convince them to spend money, when they can just cut a YouTuber for 500 pounds with more viewership, and they can track the clicks and directly see how much money they're getting back? You can't do that with just a website.

Before Instagram, before social media, before YouTube, all this came along and killed many things. Netflix. Who even watches TV channels now? That business wouldn't last anymore. I bet if you told blacksmiths 200 years ago that being a blacksmith isn't going to ever work again, they'd be like, "What? People always need metal. What are you talking about?" Blacksmiths aren't around anymore. Every single business is going to fail sooner or later. So if it's going to fail, make sure you get that money before it blows up.

I have no problem with any of my businesses going under if it's already paid me. If all my businesses fail, but I have three million, good.

If I've taken all that three million and invested it in a big studio and reinvested all the money... The goal of a business is to make you rich. This is the point of your business, to make you rich. The point of a business is not to have a business for vanity. The point of the business is to make you rich. Look after yourself first.

Obviously, this is an equation. I'm not saying only look after yourself, don't look after your business. I'm saying take this in mind, keep it as a happy equation, and make sure you're getting that money. With the agency, I made a mistake. I kept funneling all the money back into keeping the ship afloat on the waves, and I didn't take enough of the money for myself. Kept investing in new staff, new computers, dumb shit. I was 22. All the lessons I'm telling you now are lessons I've learned. If I would have just taken the money... you know what, get a deal, all right? Yeah, we'll keep it going. Yeah, just take the money, take the money, take the money! You take the money. By the time it blew up, I would be sitting on 500 grand, and I didn't. You have to look after yourself. A business won't last forever. So you have to take the money and get rich. Look after yourself.

If you're thinking about, "Oh, maybe I need a new camera, maybe I need a new car, maybe I need new vans..." Whatever your business is, doesn't matter. Think about it, but also think long and hard: Is that going to bring new money in? You need to be getting rich from your company. Look after yourself first. Because when your company fucks up, you need to be able to say, "Okay, abandon ship with money suitcases." Don't abandon it like me. When I abandoned the agency, I had nothing, and that was a mistake. I worked my ass off, sleepless nights, millions of dollars to the bank for nothing. Don't do that. Look after yourself first.

This is point 13. A business won't last forever. You need to get rich quick, and you need to take the money. Take the money for yourself. Don't run a business for vanity. Look after yourself. Get that money and keep it. If you have to choose between you and the company, most of the time, you should be choosing you. Obviously, it's a balance. You need to make sure your companies look after you. You need to reinvest in your company, of course. But still, you are the primary focus of your universe. Everything serves you, including your company.

That's point 13.

Don't make the mistake I made with my first agency, putting it all back in, and not looking after yourself. When the big banks went bust, all the banking directors, you think they didn't take big money? When the big banks all fucked up, you think they didn't take their big bonuses first? The smart people know: Look after yourself first, look after the business second. The smart people know that because as long as you're financially okay, as long as your bills are paid, your mortgage is paid, you have money, everything's going to be fine.

Lesson Fourteen: Reputation Control

I get a lot of questions from people saying, "What about my reputation? People are saying bad things." To control your reputation is very, very simple: You need to do more good than bad. You're never going to have people 100% happy, but as long as in general, you do more good than bad, you'll be okay.

In business, no matter how bad things are going, you never ignore them, even if they're blowing up your email and messaging you nonstop. "I'm unhappy! I'm unhappy!" Try to find a solution. People only get worse, they only get bitter, if they're ignored.

Because if they're emailing you, then they're not writing all over blogs and forums and making their complaints public. They're complaining directly to you, which means you can manage it. So this is another very important thing about business.

Everything I've taught you so far, you've obviously seen there were some struggles along the way. And I learned the most important thing you can do to manage your reputation is to take all the criticism personally. So they can't spend the criticism anywhere else.

If someone has any kind of problem, contact them. Say, "Hey, you got a problem, let's talk about it. See if we can work something out." Even if they're a complete unreasonable idiot, if you continue to email them back and forth, and let them vent a little, they're very unlikely to continue to just spread crap all over the internet.

Because that's the world we live in now. It's easy to find customers with the internet, it's easy to lose customers with the internet. So for reputation control, make sure you're prepared to speak to people, even when they're being weird. That's point 14.

Lesson Fifteen: Think About Money All the Time

Alright, listen up, because this is a mental game-changer. You're about to learn something huge.

I've mentioned this on Twitter before, but if you missed it, this is crucial. You have to change the way you think about money.

You're going to change where you think about money by only thinking about money all the time. I'll give you an example. 99% of people who go into a coffee shop, go in, buy coffee, sit down. If I go into a coffee shop, I go in, I look at the prices of the coffee, I look at how busy the place is, I buy my coffee, I sit down, and then I think, "If I had to run this business, would I make money? Could I run this business and make more money? How much do I think the rent is in this establishment? How much are these coffees? How busy is it here? Do they sell cakes and sandwiches to make extra revenue? Who are the main customers? Well, it's mainly businessmen. I can see there must be a business district across the road. Why are the waitresses, or why are the people who work here, not hot young girls to attract more men to come in? If that's the main customer, think outside the box and look. If I were to open a coffee shop right next door, could I beat them? Are these coffees expensive? Are they cheap? Are they good?"

You have to start looking at every single business you interact with.

Every single one. And see how you would compete with them, or if you had to run their business, if you believe you could make a profit. Because what you'll often find is, you'll see there are a lot of people making mistakes, and you think you could probably do better. You might be able to beat them.

You need to sit there, and when you're going through your normal life, you're having your coffee, you're sitting in Starbucks, whatever, obviously, competing with a multinational like that is very difficult, but any business you interact with, just start training your mind to view their business like you believe it works. Everything, from rent, overheads, the product, the profit margin, whether you think you could sell more, any tips or tricks they're missing, everything from start to finish, just have a look and see if you can work it out.

You'll be surprised how much you learn about business self-taught. I do it with every bar I'm in, every restaurant I'm in, every coffee shop I go in, everything. Even simple things, even things I know nothing about, like a mechanic. I don't know anything about fixing cars, but still, I look at the amount of cars they have around. I look at how much they charge me for my time, how much the labor is, how much I think they're charging the low-level workers. Where's the big boss? How much is he making? You need to start thinking about money and thinking about businesses like this every time you interact with one. You need to analyze it, and your analysis will get better, and you'll get more precise. Obviously, there's some information you don't know. You don't know exactly what the rent is. You can estimate it. You should be able to estimate it.

This is a really important mind hack. I teach anyone who wants to get serious about hustling and making money: You need to start approaching and looking at all businesses this way. Because what's going to happen is, when you eventually open your own business, there are going to be some lessons you identified, some mistakes you identified in the previous businesses that you're going to make sure you don't make. Whether you're opening a coffee shop or an online company, it doesn't matter what it is, you're going to identify the mistakes, and you're going to change them.

So even next time you buy something online, you buy something online. Most websites nowadays are extremely streamlined, but still, if you identify a problem with the website, if you identify a problem with the email that comes afterward, if you're unhappy with a particular aspect of customer support, if you don't like the packaging it comes in, whatever, analyze everything, and remember everything, because you're going to use this stuff for your new company.

This is a very important mind hack. This is something you need to do permanently, as a matter of habit. It's what rich people do when they're sitting around, money being made, or they're sitting around, money being exchanged. Because money's never made, money's only exchanged. When they're sitting around, and they see money being exchanged, they work out exactly how and why and who's benefiting. This is something you need to start doing as a matter of habit. It's extremely important.

Lesson Sixteen: Work Your Job Better

Alright, listen up, because this is about to get real. We're talking about the hustle, even if you're stuck in a job right now.

If you're working a job, you need to identify all the ways in which you can do your job better. A lot of people work their jobs, and they don't try very hard. We've discussed this already about how lazy employees are. If you're an employee right now, you're probably lazy.

So you're working your job, you're not trying your best. Make a list of all the ways you could improve how you do your job. You could work faster, you could make more phone calls, you could do the entire nine hours without super long bathroom breaks where you disappear to sit on your phone, whatever, whatever. Make a list of all the ways you can improve the way you do your job, then ask yourself why you don't do it. Why don't you work at 100% of your capacity?

The main reason is probably going to be because

you're not incentivized to do so. I don't know about your job, obviously, but if you're in a job right now, and the fastest way you can get a pay rise or increase your money is literally just to sit there and think, "I need XYZ to be incentivized to do this job properly..."

If you have a job right now, don't quit your job. People say to me all the time, "Oh, I need to quit my job." No, you don't. You don't need to quit your job. I guarantee there's enough time in the day for you to work your job and work your side hustle. Guaranteed. Because you're lazy and you don't do your job anyway, you have all the time you need. Continue with your job, get your side hustle rolling.

When your side hustle is rolling, and you know the money's coming in, then quit. You don't need to quit your job at the same time. So people say to me all the time, "Well, should I quit my job?" The answer is often no. You don't need to quit your job until you've been through and you've sorted out all the things we've already gone over so far in this book.

Money coming in? Why would you quit your job? Is money coming in? Yes or no? No? Well, then why would you quit your job? I showed you already how easy it is to get money flowing in. Get the site online, get the money in, even if none of the fulfillment is ready. So if money's not coming in, you don't need to quit your job. No, you need to do everything at the same time. You can get money rolling in first before you consider getting out of a job, sitting around at home, and being broke.

So that's a very important key thing about jobs, because I get asked that all the time.

Lesson Sixteen: Don't Compete on Price

Alright, listen up, because this is a crucial mindset shift. You're about to learn why competing on price is a loser's game.

People, I'm going to make this very, very clear: People do not buy on price. You do not want to compete on price, for whatever company you're going to run. You do not want to compete on price. I'll tell you why.

The people who compete on price are going to be you. So if you go to Amazon.com and look at phone cases for 89 cents for the case and delivery, and it's coming all the way from China, how do they make money on that? Do you have any clue? I don't. But they managed to pull it off. There's too much Southeast Asia and Asian production now. Everyone's producing everything so cheap. There's no way you're going to win on price.

You need to sell on brand. Here in the West, living where we live, that's our advantage. We have the whole idea of branding, quality, and reputation.

These are the things you need to sell on. You do not want to sell on price. I see a lot of guys, especially the Twitter gurus, loads of them are selling eBooks for like $17 or $13. How are you going to get rich off $17 eBooks? You're not.

If that's the only price people will buy from you at, then that shows your brand has no strength, no reputation. Because you have genuine strength and reputation, you can sell at a real price.

Where your price point lies says a lot about who you are as a person. Do you want to be Lambo or or a some broken car, all right, or do you want to be shit? I sell for a much higher margin, a much higher price, because I have a reputation, and I provide a better quality product.

So when you're looking for whatever you're going to do, whenever you're going to launch, when you start putting prices out there, if you put it up high and you're not selling, and you find yourself really reducing the price to try and get sales, that says a lot about who you are, your reputation. You need to do some reputation management, you need to build your reputation. Build your credibility. Build on the point that you're an expert in your field.

As you do that, your price will increase. That's the easiest way to make more money. Because there's only a certain amount of customers in the world. Let's say there's only a hundred who are going to buy a book about how to be good at cooking today. There's only 100 of them. That's the only people on Twitter who are going to buy a book about...

So the easiest way to make more money is to charge those hundred people more money, instead of trying to find more people. Especially with Twitter, because if you're selling on Twitter, Twitter following doesn't grow that fast. Your Twitter followers may not be that big, and even if it is, let's say an amount of 30,000, they don't grow very quickly. You get shadowbanned, takes a long, long time. So you only have a certain amount of potential customers, so you want each one to spend as much money as possible. This is the reality of the game.

So if you're selling cheap like a lot of these Twitter guys do, that's because they're cheap. You'll have more problems and more complaints from people who buy cheap things. The people who buy expensive things... and the reason is because the people who buy expensive things are getting Lambo quality, like you're getting here. All the information I'm giving you, the people who buy the cheap things, they're just buying it because it's so cheap. They don't believe in the person. They're just like, "Oh, what's the worst that can happen? I'm only losing 13 bucks." But then they'll still feel pissed off when they realize it's garbage.

So your number one goal, your number one aim in whatever business you do, is to constantly be increasing prices. You should be looking to constantly increase the price, and the way you do that is by constantly building on your reputation. That's how it goes. Even if you have to start off at a lower price, you need to always increase the price. You should never get to a point where you've priced yourself out. People don't buy on price. People buy what they want. If people want something, they're going to buy it. There's a whole bunch of expensive shit that people buy, trust me, because they want it.

So you have to make sure that people want your product. Do not be one of those "Well, I'm the cheapest on the market" guys, because that never works well. It gives you a bunch of customers, and it stops you from making any kind of serious money.

Lesson Seventeen: Shut Up and Listen

Alright, this is a game-changer. You're about to learn one of the biggest secrets to success, and it's all about shutting up and listening.

This is a really important point for business, super important, because it's something I see a lot of people make mistakes with. Most people, once they start a business, won't shut the fuck up about their business. I know so many people who are making money, yeah, they're making money, but as soon as you start talking about money, all they talk about is how they make money, their business, how smart they are, ego investment, how great they are. That's not going to teach you anything. You only learn by listening.

So whenever I'm around people who are making money, I don't talk about money. I mean, it's different if they're friends of mine, I've known them for a long time, we're interacting, but I mean, if I'm meeting people, and they're businessmen, and everyone's talking about how they're making money, I shut the fuck up and I listen.

Because anyone who's making money, one way or another, knows something you don't know. There's a lesson everywhere. So when you interact with someone who's rich, you have to say enough to convince them to talk, but don't talk too much yourself. The more you talk about your own business and how you do things, the more time you've wasted. You already know your own business. You already know how you do things. Maybe if you're asking him directly for feedback, yeah, "I do this, what do you think of this?" But if you're bragging, "I'm this, and I turn over this..." you're just wasting time. Let other people talk. Learn from other people who are making money, even if they're in an industry that's completely different to yours, it doesn't make a difference. Shut up and listen, because somebody knows something.

There's nobody you cannot learn from. You can learn from anybody who understands anything about either sales or making money. So be prepared to shut the fuck up when you interact with these people, and sit and listen, and adopt it. Be super prepared.

Lesson Eighteen: Attention is Free Advertising

Alright, listen up, because this is the fuel that makes your business engine roar.

You need to get good at getting attention. You need to find a way to get attention, because all advertising is is buying attention, which is fine, but buying attention is more expensive than getting attention for free.

I want to say, "for free," I mean free financially. To get attention is still going to take time, and it's still going to take your effort, but you need to find a way to get attention for free. I think you already understand this, you already understand viral marketing. There's no such thing as bad press. But finding a way to get attention is a fantastic way to start generating money.

Now what most people do is, you see a lot of people, they find ways to get attention, but they don't monetize it. One of my friend, he wraps cars, and he's in an industrial state, and he painted the entire side of his wall with a huge mural, like a spray paint mural of a car being wrapped. I said to him, "That was badass. How much did it cost?" He goes, "It cost me 3,000, but it's increased my business big time. I've made all my money back big time." I was like, "Why?" Because people look at it when they drive past them, and they want to, they see it as artistic, as creative, and they want to work with them.

Got attention? You painted his wall. Anything it takes to get attention. If you have a sign on your company, is your sign big and bright and bold enough? Probably not. There is no such thing as bad attention. The world we live in now, we live in an attention economy. If you have lots of attention, you can turn that into money. If you have no attention, you're not going to have any money. We're in an attention economy. You don't even need good ideas now. YouTube has proven the attention economy. You have people out there doing nothing on vlogs, talking about nothing, but because people watch it, because they get attention, they're millionaires.

Attention is the currency of the modern world. So if you're going to start any kind of business, one thing you need to consider is, we talked earlier about money in, all your money out. This is your only real business, the money in, and how you don't want to be investing any of your money in anything that doesn't lead back to more money. If you can see that bottom one there, but you know what's going to lead to this, you know it's going to increase the number of sales coming in? Attention! Attention is key. Attention is going to accelerate everything.

So you need to keep that in mind. Don't be afraid to do things that are a little bit crazy to get people to pay attention to you. Now, obviously, I'm not saying join in crimes or something stupid to get attention. Keep it in mind, but attention is the currency. Attention is the magic formula, the catalyst that's going to take any company and rise it up fast. So keep that in mind when you're looking to launch your company, or you're already running your company. "Does my company get enough attention? No? Okay, so which company in my industry does get attention? This one. How do they get it? Oh, well they pay for advertising, or for example, they did this viral campaign, or they sponsored this. Well, are the people taking the attention that you want? How can you get that attention?" Find a way! If you have to go and run a marathon dressed as a dinosaur with your company name on the back, then go do it. It's effectively free, and it's good for you. Don't be lazy. You have to do something to get some attention.

Attention is the key, that's going to be the difference between a failed business and a successful business.

Lesson Nineteen: Play on People's Insecurities

Alright, this is a lesson that's going to make you a real hustler, and it's about tapping into the dark side

People have vices, and people have insecurities. And if you can find a way to twist them, you're going to make money, even if you're running a very traditional business. Let's say you're running a clothing store. People like to feel good-looking and attractive. You have to twist that angle. You have to put something on that angle, so people go, "You know, I want to be attractive, I want to be good-looking, I want to look important, I want to be seen as important." That's what all these brands do. Porsche and Mercedes, they advertise as a businessman: "Mr. Businessman, getting in his car, he's got his briefcase, Mr. Business, he's important. You're not important, you're not a Porsche, you're a nobody, you're a loser."

You have to play to people's insecurities. You have to play on people's insecurities, and you have to find out exactly what people want.

I don't know what you're going to sell, and it doesn't matter what you're going to sell. What are you going to sell? Why do people want it? Right now, you're reading this book because you want it, because you want to learn how to make money. That's why. So in all of my advertising, and all of everything I'm doing, I make it very, very clear to you: You need this to learn how to make money. I know more about business than you, I've run more businesses than you have. If you don't get what I have, if you don't get this book, you're not going to know what I know. So you're not going to make money like I make money.

I identified the need. It's the product we have here. I identified the reason you're buying it, and I'm pushing it, pushing it, pushing it.

So I don't know what you're going to sell. Say you're selling protein shakes. I don't know, you don't sell a lot. People will sell a protein shake, "Best flavor, this much carbs, this much sugar,blah blah blah." Who cares? It's boring. If you're going to sell your protein shake, you need to say to people, "You won't be strong without the protein shake.You won't be fit without my product. Why are you wasting your time in the gym when you're not going to get in good shape anyway? Oh, you'll get in shape, but you'll be in better shape if you use my product. The product, who cares what's in the product? Sell the result. You need this, you need this because of XYZ." It doesn't matter if you're selling protein shakes, or hospitals, or universities, or raspberries. Doesn't matter what it is, you have to push that point over and over and over again. Play on people's insecurities. That's what makes people buy, because they're not going to buy otherwise.

"Oh, I could go to the gym, and I'll get in shape, and oh, do I need more carbs? I don't know. Who cares?" It's all bullshit. The odd geek will care, but most people don't care. You need protein shakes, or your gym time is a waste of time. Why are you suffering in the gym for no reason? If you drink this one drink, you're not wasting your time anymore. Stop being a loser, quickly buy it. That's how you have to be. Play on people's insecurities all the time.

Lesson Twenty: Network is Everything

Alright, listen up, because this is how you build a winning team. And it starts with who you hang out with.

I'm going to make this extremely clear to you: If you're a loser and you're rolling with losers, you are going to stay a loser. I don't even need to say that. You're going to stay a loser. Losers roll with losers, and winners roll with winners. Number 20, network is everything.

The people around you need to be thinking about money, thinking about hustling. If they're not, you don't need to talk to them. I hear this all the time: "Oh, but he's my friend, we like hanging out." Hanging out to do what? Play video games? Make jokes? Ha ha, he's so funny. If your friends aren't talking about money, why are you talking to them?

You need a network around you. You need people on your phone who are talking about money and doing important things. You need to be mixing with them. That needs to be your network. If you're rolling with a bunch of video game-playing losers, you're going to stay a video game-playing loser. This is super important. Your network has to change if you want to really become a hustler. Everyone around you needs to have a hustle.

Even if all the people around you don't have hustles, remember what I said earlier about finding free staff? Okay, let's say all your friends are losers, well now you've got a brilliant idea. So now you're the leader. "I want to run this company. You're going to do this, you're going to do this, you're going to do this." If they all sit there and go, "No, I'm tired. I don't have time." Then these people are completely useless. They're wasters. Get rid of them. They either agree to work for you, or leave them. Find some new friends.

I don't answer the phone to broke boys. You call my phone, if I answer, that dude's important. When broke boys call me, it gets ignored. All rich people are the same. I cannot stand being around people who are not on a mission to get rich. That is the only mission I'm interested in. Everyone I hang around with is on the same mission. We ain't got time for no dumb shit. So if you're still participating in dumb video games, you have got to change your mindset.

Absolutely.

If your network's full of losers, employ them. If they refuse to work for you, leave them off. Find new friends.

Lesson Twenty-One: Don't Be Overexcited

Alright, listen up, because this is about controlling your emotions and staying hungry. It's about being a cold, calculating machine when it comes to money.

Too many people get excited about a business they ain't got, or excited about a business they do have. This is just monetary exchange, gentlemen. You have to be a professional. James Bond might enjoy having girls, but you don't see him excited about it. He enjoys it, but he ain't excited. He's smooth. He's cool. He's never giddy about it.

You launch your business, you start to see some money coming in. Money's coming in, you're making some sales. Good. Be happy. Be proud of yourself, but don't be giddy. "Oh wow!" Don't be going to see clients like, "I can't wait, I really want to work, it's going to be so much fun."

This is numbers on the screen, gentlemen, that's all this is. Numbers on a screen. You're moving numbers around. Learn some emotional control. Don't be getting all giddy. I don't know why I wrote that down, but that's the basic lesson here. I see so many people get giddy and excited: "Oh, we might get this much money!" One, you haven't got the money yet. Two, even if you've got the money, good. All you have to do... do you know what you have to do when money comes in the door? Let me tell you, because maybe you don't know. This is me. Here's money coming into the door on Tuesday. On Wednesday, do you know what I do? I wake up, and I try to find some more money. Don't worry about it. Don't be getting excited about money, because when money comes in, You're allowed two or three seconds of excitement when you check the bank, then it doesn't exist anymore. It's past? Okay, past, now it's done. This is done, it's in, it's done, it's gone. Even if I still save it, it's effectively gone. You have to find a way to make more. You shouldn't be getting excited about big chunks of money, or any chunks of money. You should always be pushing for more, and more, and more, and more, and more.

Don't be excited about what you've already achieved. You can't live in the past. Living in the past is going to sink your business. You have to live in the future, constantly pushing for more.I wake up every day broke, every day. I wake up at zero, poor every day, no matter how much money I've made the day before. That's not how I operate. Every day is a new day. You wake up broke.

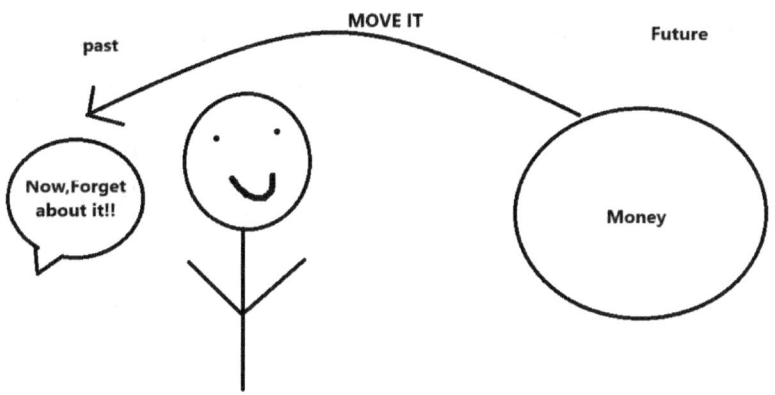

Don't be getting giddy and excited and emotional. "Oh, but last week, we had a really good week." Who cares? That was last week. Iran hadn't attacked an American army base in Iraq last week. Last week was a different world. This is this week, shit's different. Don't be getting excited about old shit. Every single day, you are poor. Every single day, you need to attack and go again. Every single day from...zero you have to start, every day you wake up at zero. Don't be getting giddy and excited and emotional about money you've already made, or money you might make, which is even worse.

I used to know so many sales guys when I worked with me, so many sales guys would be in the office, laughing, drinking their coffee, talking, saying, "Oh, I've got four really good leads. I've got four really good pitches. Uh, they should be coming in today." Laughing about money they thought was coming in, that they hadn't made yet. And even if all four came in (which had never happened), two came in, even if four came in, the time they're wasting being happy about it, they could have found more.

Don't waste time counting money that you ain't got yet, or counting money you've already got. You live right now, in the present. Right now, in the bank, even if it's 10 million dollars, it doesn't matter, it's over, it's finished. You should never be looking that way. You should always be chasing more, and more, and more, and more, and more. And you should be living here, in the present. When I say chasing, I don't mean excited for, I mean you need to get it from the future, move it to the past, and forget about it. More, more, more, more, more.

If I have a really, really good day with the agency, and all the clients were happy, and we made 12, 13 thousand dollars in a day profit for me, the next day,

I'd wake up and say, "Yesterday's done. Yeah, it was a good day, but it's over. Today is a new day. Today, you're on zero." "Oh, but yesterday, we made so much." Yesterday? I don't live in yesterday. I live in today, and the only day that's coming for me is tomorrow. Yesterday is gone. You have to be that way with money. So many business people will do a little bit of business, and sit on their ass. There's some guy on Twitter going, "Oh, I had a really bad year, I took my foot off the gas." Did you want to teach people about business? And he's saying publicly on Twitter that he made a little bit of money, so he became a lazy piece of shit, and then his money ran out, or his business fell apart, and now he's broke. You dumb, lazy...

So he can sit around in his apartment, like, "What's wrong with people?" More, more, more. Next, next, next. I don't care how big of a deal you do, I don't care how many clients you closed online. I don't care what happened yesterday. It's over. You have to push forward at all times. I've seen so many people do a little bit of business, and end up changing their attitude to money. "Oh, I've got some money now." No, you don't have that. That's yesterday's money.

Lesson Twenty-Two: Send People Their Money Back

Alright, listen up, because this is a business hack that's going to blow your mind. It's something I learned that nobody does, and it works brilliantly.

Check this out. My business hack is... drumroll... send people their money back. They love it.

How many times have you bought something, and you really wanted it, but then you kind of looked at your bank afterward, and thought, "Um, that was expensive. What a bit of a waste of money." You know what I mean?

So what I used to do when I sold advertising was, I had this trick where I'd sell a package, let's say I don't know, 2,000. They'd buy it. I'd sell it, they'd buy it, say bye. When the invoice came in, I'd call them up and go, "Hey, uh, I just want to let you know that some things have changed. I don't think now is the optimal time for you to start your advertising. I'm interested in this as much as you are. I have a vested interest in this working. I don't want to just take your money. I want to make sure that this pays off for both of us.

Because if it pays off for both of us, we do a lot of business in the future. I think it'd be better to wait about two weeks. In two weeks from now, things will be a better opportunity. So what I'm going to do is, I'm going to send you your money back now. I don't want to steal your money. It's your money. We can still do the campaign. I just think if we wait a week, maybe two, not very long, I think there'll be some more opportunities in the market."

They'd be like, "Oh, okay. Yeah, alright."

That's what you think. I said, "Yeah, I want this to work. I've been doing this a long time. I want to make sure this is very good for both of us." Blah blah blah. And I'd send them their money back, and they'd be like, "What the fuck? I tried to buy it, and he gave me my money back." It's kind of like a takeaway, you know, the takeaway trick. I tried to buy it, and he said no, and he gave me my money back. And now they trust you loads because no one gives refunds, no one gives money back. So he gave me my money back, then when I called him a week later, and said, "Bang, now it's time to do business. I've got a fantastic opportunity. We're going to do this, we're going to do

this. We have this gap, we have that gap. No, no, no,

No, no, no, it's only 3,000." Every time they buy, they're like, "Oh, that's more. So yeah, I know it's more than last time. I mean, we can do the 2,000 package now, but there's a really good opportunity here."

You build so much trust when you send the money back that they will spend more later. I did this trick with every customer. Every client would buy, pay, call them up. "Now's not the right time." Send them their money back. Talk about how I'm really looking after them, how I want a really good relationship. And then hit them up for a bigger invoice every time, and it always worked. It works because the trust you build when you send someone their money back is immense because no one does that. Nobody does that. Remember what I said earlier about there being only 100 people on Twitter who want to buy an eBook? It's the same with everything.

So my logic was this: If you're selling $17 eBooks, let people buy it for $17, email them, and say, "You know what, I'm going to update the eBook now, so I'm going to send you your money back. I'm sending your money back because the eBook's going to be updated. I want you to have the most updated version. Here's your..." Let me know how to pay you.

Email them personally, so they have to see it and reply. Don't just click refund. They might not know it's us. Let them look at that and go, "Okay, oh yeah, okay. Send the money here." Send them their $17 back. Then they'd be like, "Okay, that was weird." Then email them again. "Hey, let you know, working on the update, it's going to be out soon. I think you're really going to like it." I could have... and then remind them, "I could have left you with the older version, but I think it'd be better to have the most up-to-date stuff. Bang." Email them again.

Watch that person go, "Oh yeah, you know, I really appreciate that. Most people wouldn't do that. Most people wouldn't care." Because now you've sent them their money back. This person... you don't understand the psychological effect this has on people. Now they're like, "Whoa, I can trust this dude." Then you come at them, and go, "Hey, so it's updated. I've updated. I'm going to give you the latest version, as well as that. I've got a new product that's coming out. It's not out yet. It's blah blah blah. It's worth $100. If you're interested in both, I'll give you both for $40. Bang!" I guarantee you he buys it. You've turned a

$17 sale into a $40 sale with a two-day wait and two emails. You've doubled your turnover! You've doubled your turnover. Do you have any idea how important that is? You've doubled your turnover by... with a two-day wait and a couple of emails.

Lesson Twenty-Three: Hard Close

Alright, listen up, because this is how you turn prospects into paying customers. It's about being assertive and closing the deal.

Now, a lot of people already understand this. This is why they do false urgency: "Buy now, running out of time." But you have to hard close people because people don't buy things without being hard closed. You have to find a way to close them. You either have to do the false urgency thing, "We're running out of time," or you can just do... you can do, "If you don't buy now, it's going to be very hard to get this deal later on." Now, everyone knows this. This is very basic sales.

But in my experience, I've tried soft closing, and I've tried hard closing. Hard closing is better. With hard closing, you lose some people, but the people you close outweigh the people you lose. I see so many businesses just working softly, just waiting for people, waiting, waiting, waiting. It's better to go hard and just get the business done, or not. You have ten potential leads. If you have ten potential leads, it's better to hard close. Come in, come in like Rambo, close five, and lose five. That's sitting there on ten that might drop in, might not drop in, because that ten that might drop in, might not drop in, fucks with you, with your estimated numbers. It's like, "Oh, maybe tomorrow will have money." It wastes your time. No, blow up the water. Get some definite. A definite is better than a maybe.

Get a definite. Some people go, "Oh, I've got this maybe. This maybe, this maybe, this maybe." Why are they maybes? Make a phone call right now!, and close the deal.

Lesson Twenty-Four: It Ain't Real 'Til They Pay

Wait, wait, we're on number 24. We're almost a quarter of the way through! Think how much you've learned in this book. We're a quarter of the way through. 24. It ain't real 'til they pay. And I mean money in the bank.

So when I was running my first agency, I had the chance to land a deal for a company. They were a very big company. A junior marketing manager convinced our agency was a fantastic idea. We're talking about sponsorships. Anyway, this was a 600,000 pound deal with a quarter of a million pounds profit for me. They wanted to do business. I sent them the proposed advertising plan, they loved it. Sent them the contract, they loved it. The deal was done. And when I say done, I know you don't count money until it's in the bank, but it was done. They'd emailed back, "Yes, no problem. We've signed the contract. The deal is done. We were just waiting for the money to show in the bank. Anyway, so we're emailing, emailing, emailing the head of marketing. She got sick. So when you emailed her, it came back saying, "Hi, on unexpected leave. Disease, whatever." She got sick. The junior marketing manager had no power, and it turns out the big managing director didn't want to start the campaign when the marketing manager was away. So he just wouldn't pay the invoice. Stop them? Sue them? Because he knew they were so big, this is like a billion pound company. We couldn't sue them, like, I know they signed the contract, what are we really going to do about it? Like, we're just me and my staff, are we going to take him to court? Waste our time and money?

So we're sitting there, waiting for money, and guess what? It never comes. Until the money's in the bank, it ain't real. It doesn't matter if they signed the contract, it doesn't matter if they said yes, it doesn't matter if they agree to everything, it doesn't matter if you've started the work, nothing matters until the money is in the bank. This is super important, because when we realized the money wasn't coming, that was the closest I've ever come to feeling genuine depression in a very long time. We were so excited about that money. We did exactly what I said don't do. We got giddy. We weren't professional. We were excited. Quarter of a mil liquid cash! What can we do? We can do this, we'll go there, or die by this. But change our lives. All this. We weren't rich then. This is life-changing money.

Do not get excited about money totals that are not in the bank. Super, super important. Because trust me, that fucked me up for like a week. I couldn't even work properly for a week. So pissed off, totally demotivated. Don't let that happen to you, and that feeds into the next part.

Lesson Twenty-Five: Stress Tolerance

You need to learn to care about things mentally, but not emotionally. How successful you are as a hustler is directly linked to how much stress you can tolerate. Money-making is only stress tolerance.

So when you're making money, most of the time, what you're doing is you're taking stress off other people. Especially if you provide a service. You run a cleaning service? You're taking stress away from someone else. You're adopting someone else's stress for cash. The more stress you can adopt, the more money you can take.

You need to have high stress tolerance as a hustler, as a money-maker, as a businessman. You have to be able to deal with stress. Things are going to go wrong all the time. You have to be able to just ride the waves.

So in life, usually, there are two kinds of people: You have the stoner who smokes, doesn't give a fuck about anything, who gets nowhere. And you have the person who cares about things, but it's very emotional very uptight. "Oh, sake! Oh no, this has gone wrong!" Angry, running around like a nutcase. You don't want to be either of them. You want to be in the middle. You have to care about things mentally, but not emotionally.

The website's gone down, and PayPal has blocked us, and whatever, whatever, whatever. You need to sit there and go, "Okay, alright. I understand. Let's find a solution." And you need to care mentally, but not be getting emotional about it. Stress tolerance is a huge aspect of this. Mostly, people out there, the only reason you're not successful is because you can't tolerate stress. And I'm saying this to you now, you cannot tolerate stress.

"What do you mean? I know I can!"

I know you can't, because if you could, you'd already have side businesses. And you don't. You work a job, and you don't have side businesses because, "Oh, I'm busy, I'm tired." This is sales stress tolerance. Needing to sleep is stress. That shows you have a low stress tolerance. Not having the energy shows you have a low stress tolerance. Not knowing what to do, it's a low stress tolerance. You do know what to do. You have ideas. You're just lazy, and you're just afraid of the effort, and you don't like the idea of stress. "Oh, now I've got more things to do, I can't handle it." More things? You're a little baby. Stress tolerance is super important. Life's stressful. Being successful is stressful. I have three supercars on the drive, and it's all stress to get them, and I enjoy them when I drive them. And I wouldn't have it any other way.

You have to increase your stress tolerance. You're going to be stressed. You have to learn to do more things and deal with more shit. Increase your stress tolerance. If you're watching this right now, I don't care what position you're in. Start a company today, and deal with it. The quicker you get better at swimming through it, the quicker you're going to get through it to the end, which is money.

Stress tolerance is super, super important. I can't stress that enough.

Lesson Twenty-Six: Sell the Need, Not the Product

I kind of touched on this earlier with the protein shake. But it's an important point. How do you sell protein shakes? You convince people they need them. This is one of the most basic tenets of business. You have to convince people they need whatever you sell. You don't talk about the product, you talk about their need.

What's the old adage they do? "Sell me this pen." You ever heard that before? "Sell me this pen." People go, "Oh, well, this pen is blue, and this pen is uh... it's made of plastic, and it's durable." No, it's not that. That's not how you sell a pen. "Sell me this pen." You need to be able to write things down. But I've already got a pen. Yeah, but now you can write more things down. You have another pen. How are you going to write down all your ideas? Think of all the things you can write down. You can write the next novel. You can become J.K. Rowling. You can become a billionaire, if you had a pen. You don't have a pen, you need a pen to write things down.

Sell the need. Don't sell the product. "It's blue, and it's plastic," as opposed to, "You can become J.K. Rowling because you need a pen to write things down."

You have to sell the need at all times. Most people don't sell the need. I sold you the need. You need to know what I know about business. It's the need that sells, not the product.

So whatever you're selling, it doesn't matter what it is. Sell the need. Even if you're selling raspberries. They need raspberries. "Why do I need raspberries?" You need raspberries because it's good for your, I don't know, immune system. Talk about superberries. Sell the need at all times. You will catch yourself not selling the need, all the times. You'll catch yourself not selling the need.

So even a coffee shop, this is the biggest mistake things like coffee shops make. They don't sell the need. They'll sell on a coffee shop, they'll sell you on price. They'll try and do it nice and cheap, because they have lots of competition. They'll sell... they'll have a nice-looking coffee shop. They'll have like a good, you know, nice chairs, that'll look nice, whatever. But they very rarely sell the need.

If I had a coffee shop, I would have a massive sign outside saying, "Tired? Nice warm coffee." The need! Because everyone's tired, aren't they? Everyone's stressed, everyone's going through life tired a bit. "Nice warm coffee?" Yeah, nice warm coffee, okay, walk in. That's selling the need. I don't say, "Arabica beans in a cup." No one cares. Sell the need at all times. Never take your eye off that prize.

If you're still paying attention, which you should be, write that down already. All the information I've given you should be formulating how you view business. They sometimes buy things they want, but they always buy things they need. That's why they have to need what you sell. So find a way to make them need it.

Lesson Twenty-Seven: Contracts Aren't Real

This is something that most people don't understand, in my experience of business. If you're going to be a hustler, if you're trying to get rich, it's as follows: Until you're a big rich company, or until you have lots of money in the bank, contracts are not real. Legal paperwork is not real. None of these things are real. Look at the earlier company example. They signed the contract. They owed me that money. If I would have taken them to court, I would have spent a lot of money, and would they have paid me in the end? No.

None of these things are real. Do you know why legality isn't real? Because legality defies rule number one of this book. What's rule number one? Rule number one is speed. And guess what lawsuits are? Slow. Super slow. And if you're a new business, you do not have time to be suing people. It's going to take forever. Years, years for a maybe. And even if you do get a yes, they can still delay for years. If they even pay you, which they probably won't. It's different if you're like suing a huge news outlet or something. In general, you want to do your business based on trust and cash. You don't want to be having, "Oh, I don't really trust all the contracts. Well, I've got the contract. I've got the contract." If they don't want to pay you, they're not going to pay you. A contract... what are you really going to do about it?

I am not a fan of contracts. I don't work with contracts. I don't like legality. It's very, very slow. So if you're looking to start your business, you're like, "Okay, we need to contract with this person, contract with that person." You know what's better than contracts? Mutual interest. It's good for me if I do my part, it's good for him if he does his part. Look at how a road works. You're driving down the road. Why do they not crash into each other? Well, it's good for him if they don't crash. It's good for him if they don't crash. Nobody wants to crash, so we all avoid it. Isn't that better than having a contract saying, "We won't crash." Then he does crash into me. Well, I have the contract, but the crash has already happened, and everything's a mess.

Mutual interest. Find a way to do business with people with mutual interest. My suppliers, I don't need a contract from my supplier because they want me to buy things from them. What contract for what? I see so many people who get involved in business start talking about contracts because they like to sound smart. Very much like we were talking about earlier on about people who like to spend money at the beginning, and get their logo, and spend money and get a big backend, and all this.

They like to sound intelligent. That's not business. This is business: money in. The rest ain't business. Contracts aren't business. Contracts you might have to deal with when you get bigger, but in general, don't be thinking, "If I can get in the sign of a contract, then I've got it." You haven't got anything. You've got a piece of paper, and if you try to enforce that contract, it's going to bankrupt you. So don't be relying on contracts anyway.

I see a lot of people doing that, and I don't know why. A piece of paper doesn't mean anything unless you enforce it, and enforcement is very, very slow and very, very expensive. So forget about contracts. Find a way, if you're going to have to work with another company or another person, for it to be mutual interest. Mutual self-interest keeps the traffic of the world flowing. It keeps the business world flowing, too. That whole suing each other, that's some mess. You don't want to get mixed up in that. It ain't going to get you rich. Hustlers are looking to get money.

Lesson Twenty-Eight: Make Sure Your Partners Need You

This is a very, very important one. You need to make sure your partners always need you, and you need to make sure you always need your partners. Not want, need. If you look at your partners and realize they don't need you, or you don't need them, then you should do it on your own. Stop being a coward because you can be the absolute managing director. You can find your number one employee from your old company or someone you really trust and make them your number two in command. Now you effectively have a partner.

This is another thing you don't understand, people. People want partners because they like the idea of having someone to vibe off of or work with, or someone who they can check their thinking with. That's fine if you have a partner, and you both need each other, and it's 50/50. Good. I'm not saying don't have partners. I have partners in some of my companies.

However, you can still have all the benefits of a partner with a number two in command who's loyal to you. Now you still have the benefits of a partner, but you control everything.

Make sure you need your partners, and they need you. There are lots of ways you can do that: Mutual self-interest, you can do things they can't do. You need to work together to get the job done. Otherwise, feel free to just hire someone and make sure they're your second in command, and just make them feel important, and use them to bounce your thinking. Be the only control person who's in control.

Don't get in your company, not that it's likely to happen, but still, even if you're making loads of money, you have a partner, and you don't need them now. You've got half the money you're making. Why...?

Lesson Twenty-Nine: Every Purchase is an Impulse Purchase

So if someone does eventually buy from you, even if they've been thinking about it for a long time, the moment they finally decide to pull the trigger and buy is an impulse purchase. That's why I say hard close. That's why people do false scarcity, all these things trying to get them to impulse buy. You can go and do a lot of research on impulse purchases, how they work, why people make them, etc.

Everybody, after they purchase, the time between the money leaving the bank and then receiving the product, even if it's a few milliseconds, is going to have that little bit of, "Um, that's a lot of money I just spent." Every single purchase is an impulse purchase. Remember that, keep it in mind. I've had a lot of people say to me, "Oh, you're selling impulse purchases. I don't mind, it's a considered purchase." No, no, it's an impulse purchase.

A house is an impulse purchase. A supercar is an impulse purchase. At the point of buying, it's an impulse purchase, no matter how long they consider it for. When they finally click send, it's an impulse purchase.

So all the tactics and tricks I'm teaching you to get people to impulse buy work on every single kind of sale, because every single kind of sale is an impulse purchase. Don't get stuck up in some thinking, "Oh, mine's not an impulse purchase. Mine's considered." Shut up. It's all impulse purchasing. All of it. Everybody impulse purchases.

If you look at any kind of sales tips and tricks, look at impulse purchasing, how it works, why people do it, and those are the factors you need to implement, especially when you're trying to close a considered purchase. If you've been talking to them for a long time, you're trying to close them, bang, you're trying to convince them to make an impulse purchase. It's as simple as that. All sales are impulse purchases, and they're not buying on price. Those two go together very, very well. Remember those two points. It's important.

So how does a real estate agent do that, like a house

is a considered purchase? This is where you're going to live, and it's very, very expensive. Well, they come, and they show you around. They make you want it, and then they start telling you, "Other people have wanted it, other people are viewing the house. They're going to put in an offer." Trying to force you to make an impulse, "Yes or no? Uh, uh, okay, we'll take it." They understand. Everyone understands. It's always an impulse purchase. You have to put something there to make people buy, make them do it, or they're simply not going to do it.

Do not give people open-ended timeframes. If I say, "You can have this pen today for X amount, or you can come back to me anytime and get the pen. No rush." Why would I buy now? I'll live without the pen for a while until I really need the pen. And I'm not going to need the pen unless you convince me of the need, so I'm never going to buy the pen. Everything's an impulse purchase. You have to convince someone they need it, and you have to hard close them. This is something, just understand the nature of how people sell and how people buy. Because this is the same with absolutely everything, no matter what it is

Lesson Thirty: Promise Your Clients a Future

This is important. A lot of people I see do not sell a future with their clients, and I don't understand why. You should sell a future with your clients. You should say, "Look, we're going to work together for a very long time in the future. XYZ is going to happen in the future. I'll be able to provide you with XYZ."

When you talk about the future, you presume the present. So this is a trick. When I was selling advertising, I was talking to clients, and I'm trying to close a small, 19 grand deal, I'd be talking about two years, when we're doing the 500 grand deals. So when I'm trying to close this, I'm talking about that we already are making deal in the future. I'll be like, "Oh well, in the future, well, in a few years, when we're launching the big campaigns, we can do the sponsorships, we can sponsor the before and after the programs, and when you're spending that kind of money, we'll also be able to have meetings directly with the channel." They're sitting there going, "Yeah, okay, yeah, sponsorships, yeah, yeah, yeah, yeah

yeah, yeah." Talk about all this imaginary stuff to try and close this.

Sell the future at all times. If you presume the future, it makes you more likely to buy now. And that's something that people don't do, even for $17 eBooks, for advertising, for websites. It doesn't matter what it is. If I was trying to sell a new website, I'd be talking about how two years later, down the line, we can integrate a new backend with our website. Who knows, who gives a fuck? Talk about some fancy shit that's going to happen in the future. If you do that, you're more likely to sell now. That's super important. Don't talk about now.

Lesson Thirty-one Image Sells

We're hustlers. This is the hustler's university. Image sells. Now, there are a lot of guys on Twitter who constantly talk about saving money. It grates on me. It annoys me. These are the other guys in the saving money, the making money space. It's not how much you make, it's how much you save? "Can you save, save, save? Stay at home, save. Don't have a girlfriend, she's expensive. Save, save." It's bullshit. You need to have a nice image of yourself if you want to sell things. Buy the nice car. Wear a nice suit. Find some money, make sure it's still coming in, because buying the nice car, you say, "Oh, how does that make equal money in?" Well, it actually does, because it's your reputation.

You have to have a nice image of yourself to sell nearly anything nowadays. Drive a nice car if you can. Have nice clothes. Look good. Look presentable. Go to the gym. Have nice things. I'm not going to tell you not to have nice things. A lot of people who say that are liars. They're tight losers, they're living a tight person's life. Do you really want that life? Do you want to be selling $17 eBooks, sitting at home and not spending any money, and saving it all? Go squirrel. Or do you want to be like me, with three supercars?

Who knows more, let me ask you another question. The difference between me and all the other course guys. These guys need courses to be rich. I'm rich without any of this. So I don't need this.

The reason my second comapny was so successful was because I already had a good lifestyle. I was already rich. My car paid for itself. I'm not saying blow all your money. I'm saying having a good image is not going to hurt you in any way. Don't be afraid to spend money on your image, because it's a real thing.

Lesson Thirty-Two: Learn to Speak

Everything in life is basically the same thing, talking. Everything in life is people walking into rooms and saying things. That's what politics is. That's what business is. That's what negotiations are. Everything you can think of is some guy walking into somewhere and starting to talk. That's what the Senate is. That's what Congress is. It's what court is. Everything is people talking.

Talking is something you need to get good at. If you're good at talking, you have the gift of the gab, as they say. You can sell anything, no matter what you're selling. The better you get at talking, the better you're going to sell it. So if there's one skill you need to practice for your sales, it's how to talk. How to talk convincingly. How to put energy into your presentation. How to not be boring. Learn to speak.

If you don't have my Alpha Male book, buy it right now. It teaches you body language, and we cover oration. We talk about talking, and how the way I talk, what I do, things, tips, tricks, etc.

If you want to learn to talk like me, the Grandmaster, I'll teach you. But you need to be good at speaking. Being good at speaking will make you good at selling. They are the same thing.

Get used to talking.I've seen, I've been in presentations over and over again with people who have a fantastic product, fantastic information, a great price point, but just...(THE WAY THEY TALK) and the presentation is slick, they've got the PowerPoint, etc., but they're just not good at talking. There's no X-factor with their talk. There's no vibe. You need to have that vibe. You need to get good at talking. Practice it. Practice getting good at talking. That's one of the most important skills you can learn for life. From getting women to selling products, exactly the same thing. You need to get good at talking. It's important.

There are lots of different ways you can go about talking. My way, the way I talk, suits my personality. You have to develop your own type. But I make sure I try my best to make sure I put loads of energy into how I speak. Most people speak, and they don't realize, super low energy. And then we will... and when you have the eBook, you don't sell the eBook, you sell the result of the eBook, because if you sell the eBook, you're bored already. I'm bored. So I scream, and I move my arms around, and I'm eccentric. I'm over the top. You don't have to be that way. There are other ways you can also be engaging without being the same as me. I know a lot of other guys are engaging in other ways, but you have to develop an angle to be engaging.

So next time you talk to someone who's an engaging speaker, find out why they're engaging. Even some people are engaging because they laugh all the time. People like positivity. So have you ever been around someone who's like constantly laughing when they talk? But then you're like, "Well, you listen more because what's so funny? His life seems great. I want to know what he knows."

Find a way to differentiate yourself one way or another. There are loads of different tips and tricks. I can't tell you to be like me, because I'm me, and you're you, but you need to find a way to be engaging. And the way you do that is, next time you're listening to someone and you're particularly engaged, work out what about them is engaging.

Lesson Thirty-Three: Avoid "Um"

So I like to be high energy, and high energy always helps. Being low energy never helps anything. Even if you're in bed, at least if you're high energy, it'll be better. For low energy, to do something... one thing you do need to avoid is "um, um, um, um." Everyone does it, but if you purchased my Alpha Male book, I teach how to do that in the body language section. So if you're reading this and you want to be able to speak like me, free-flowing, machine gun, get the body language module.

But you start slowly. You talk slowly, you breathe, you make sure you don't make any "ums," and then you get better at it, and you can be as quick as me. Now, I talk very, very fast, without mistakes, without gaps. "Oh, and um..." will lose you a deal. "Oh, so explain to me how the flux capacitor works. Um, um, okay, so, uh..." You just lost it. You just lost the deal right there. And 99% of people will do exactly that, even people who are good, even experienced people. "Oh, okay, so, um, uh, why? How does the flux capacitor work?"

I'm going to tell you exactly how the flux capacitor works. Here's how it works. Look at this, I just... I just got the deal. You didn't. All I did was repeat his question. You're saying "ah," so you have time to think. I'm repeating the question so I have time to think. "Tell me how the flux capacitor works. Uh, okay, uh, uh..." Or, "Tell me how the flux capacitor works." I'll tell you what I'm going to do. I'm going to tell you exactly how the flux capacitor works. All I did was repeat the question. It's not complicated. There are tips and tricks so you learn how to speak without sounding like a... boom. If someone else is in a presentation with me, I won't buy from them because I don't speak that way. Learn how to not speak that way.

If you're reading this and you want to learn what I know about how to talk, get the body language module. It'll teach you. I'll give you one little trick there, but there's a bunch more.

Lesson Thirty-Four: Everything Will Go Wrong

Everything will go wrong all the time. That's why you need to have a high stress tolerance, and that's also why you need rule number one: Your best weapon against things going wrong is rule number one, speed. Speed defies gravity. If you get water in a bucket and you spin it round really fast, the water doesn't come out of the bucket. As soon as you slow down, it falls out. Speed is that powerful. You have to be able to work quickly. You need people around you who work quickly. You need teams that react to things quickly, quickly, quickly, quickly.

Everything will go wrong all the time. The faster you can plug the hole and fix things, the faster you're going to be back online, making money. So anticipate things going wrong. High stress tolerance and speed are the remedies to all your issues, no matter what the issue is. No matter what the ailment, you need to do things quickly to get it fixed, always. As long as you can keep this going, you've got your business going.

So let's say you've got your business, money's coming in, your backend fails, your big backend all up. "Oh, no, everything's gone wrong!" Do you know what I do in that situation? Most people in that situation go, "Oh, well, we can't take orders because we can't see who, what order..." No. Not interested. My business is still running as long as my payment gateway is taking money. My business is running. I'll deal with the shit, I'll fix the shit. I'll deal with it, using rule number one, speed. But I'm not turning off my money tap. As long as this is happening, you won't go out of business, you won't lose. You will only lose when money stops.

So even if everything in your whole company's gone wrong, you're going to sleep less. You're going to get it fixed. You're going to fix it with speed. You've got a high stress tolerance, you'll deal with it. Your staff understands speed, speed, speed, speed. You're going to tear through the mess manually. You'll have to go through manually, one by one, and get it fixed. But you're not going to stop your business running this way. Your business... never, ever, ever let MONEY IN get fucked up, ever.

 If everything goes down, what's the first thing you fix? This is a test. Everything goes down. What's the first thing you get back online? How to take money. You don't care about anything else until money is online. There's nothing else without it. It's like, what's going on in your life? What's the first thing you fix? You fix oxygen. If you ain't got oxygen, the game's up. Nothing else is important. That's what this is. You fix MONEY IN. Get the payments coming in, then worry about it.

 Worst case, everything's so messed up, you can't even see what people bought. Don't worry, don't worry about it. They'll email you. "Hey, I spent money on your website, ain't got my product."

"Oh, really? Please tell me the time and date. I'm sorry about that. Here's the time and date. Okay, yeah, they did buy. Okay, confirm it. Okay, yeah. Sorry about that. We're going to send you a free gift." Apologize for the delay, bang! Problem solved. You kept your money in. You've got them happy. They've got a free gift. Wait for them to email you. Keep the money coming at all costs. Super important. Everything's going to go wrong, but as long as you keep this going, and you work quickly, you can fix the other things.

Lesson Thirty-Five: Find Loyal People, Then Find Them a Job

Everything I know about business, from start to finish, every single business I run, I run by these principles. Literally every single one of them.

If you can find a loyal person, find them a job. Most people approach recruitment like, "I have a job, I need to fill. Let me find a person." I approach recruitment the other way around. I try my best to go through life as I interact with people. If I find a person who I believe would be a good fit for my leadership style, which is, "Do whatever I say, and do it quickly," then I'll find them work. You can always find more work. The work is never done. Work is a black hole. Even if it's just to sit on my Twitter account and retweet tweets all day, it's still work, still engagement, still attention, still advertising.

If I find someone who fits my style, and I believe they'd be a good worker, and they're loyal to me, and I know I'm going to be able to count on them, I'll find work for them. Don't turn down people you think will be good because you can't find work. If you're running a business, and you can't think of work to do for an employee, then you shouldn't be running a business.

It's very easy to find work. There's always something to do. There's always Twitter to tweet on, or blogs to write, or go on Reddit and post forums, and post with links to your product. There's always something to do. If you find a good person, hire them, and find a job afterward. That's key. And then, as real jobs appear in your organization, as you grow, you'll already have loyal members of staff you can reorganize. Don't throw away loyal people.

Lesson Thirty-Six: Aim Way Too High

When I say way too high, I mean way too high. Now, don't be one of those people who comes along, going, "Yeah, I'm going to go on Moon, or some thing, or The Apprentice. I'm going to be a multi-millionaire.",okay, you will be!!, after reading this book. But don't be an idiot. But you need to aim too high. The higher you aim, the higher you'll get. If you aim for the moon, you'll get to the stars. If you aim for the stars, you'll get to the sky. If you aim for the sky, you won't get off the ground. That's how it goes.

You need to aim high. Be realistic, don't be delusional, but you do need to aim too high. Whatever your expectations are, you need to triple, at least quadruple them. Because if your product is good, and you're doing a good job, and you're selling it to the whole world, why can't you be a billionaire? Why not? If you're doing a good job and selling a good product to the whole world, why couldn't you?

So you need to aim much higher than you're currently aiming. It's going to help you reach higher levels. Just don't be one of them deluded guys who's already talking about half a million dollar turnover when he has literally sold zero.

I guess another way to phrase this lesson, number 36, is never be content. So when your money's coming in, let's say you get to the point where you're doing $2,000 a day, $1,000 a day, whatever, never sit there and go, "Oh, that's pretty good." It's never good. It's never good enough, ever. It's never enough. It's never good enough. It's never enough to make you happy. Be greedy. Want more. Aim high, all the time.

It's your instant source of motivation. If you're happy and content with what's coming in, you're not going to aim high enough. You have to be pushing forward. Remember, always look into the new money, forget the old money. Aim higher, all the time. I can't stress that enough.

Lesson Thirty-Seven: Irrational Self-Confidence

Without being a bullshitter, people like confidence. If I'm going to spend my money with you, I want you to be extremely confident in what you're doing with my money. If I'm going in for surgery, I'm going to go see a doctor for surgery. Do I want that doctor to be confident about the operation, or nervous? Do I want the doctor to say, "Yeah, I've done this loads of times. Yeah, I know exactly what we're going to do here. Yeah, it's easy. It's simple. I've done it loads of times." Or do I want him to be like, "Oh well, yeah, I mean things can go wrong, and you know... you know, I didn't sleep last night."

What do you want? You want confidence. So someone's going to spend money with you, they want you to be competent all the time. So you have to be confident in your delivery. Now, don't be a liar. You need to be super confident at all times. So if anyone's going to spend money with you, they need to be confident.

When I used to go into sales, when I would go sell things, when I was doing advertising, I would say I was the best. So I was the best. Now, I was relatively new to the game, and I'd say, "Yeah, I've been in this game a long time, I've met a lot of people, and I've met a lot of agencies to see how they do things. I'm really... I'm not... I'm not trying to sound conceited, but I'm very sure that we are the best at what we do." And they'll be like, "Oh, okay." I'm saying, "No, really, we are the best at what we do, in terms of price-wise, and the way we plan the media. I know we're the best. We're the best in the country." Did I have any evidence? No. Just said it.

"Give us evidence."

"What evidence?" They go, "Why?" And I say, "Oh, because the way we do planning and the price point we work out, I've been doing this industry a long time, I've seen lots of people, and I've also taken lots of big clients from other competitors, and I know that we're the best. Bang!" Just said it right there, and if you say it so confidently, they're not going to be like, "Well, no, you're not." They don't know. They don't know anything about your industry. How are they going to disprove it? They're like, "Oh, okay, oh well."

People love confidence. They want to give their money to the best because they know the best is going to give them the best job. It's better to be irrationally self-confident than not. This also ties into the "um" thing. Did you notice how smooth I was right then when I said why I'm the best? Did I go, "Um, I think, uh, we're the best, uh..." No. I'm the best.

Any job you do, any client you're going to land, you need to sit there and say, "I'm the best at what I do. I'm the best at what I do." What are they going to do? Say, "No, you're not." "Yeah, I am." "No, you're not." "How do you know? It's my industry, not yours. I'm telling you, I'm the best at what I do. You're not going to find anyone better than me for this price point. No way, impossible. I am the best. There's no one else in the world who does what I do at this cost. I'm the best. Congratulations, you found the best. You're lucky."

Irrational self-confidence. Do not be a bullshitter, but you need to be super self-confident. Smooth with it. James Bond, he walks in, he's outnumbered, everyone wants to kill him. "I'm the best." Doesn't matter. "I'm me, I'm a genius." That's how you have to be. Irrational self-confidence, super important. A lot of people don't have enough confidence when they're trying to sell. I don't know why. You're trying to sell something, and you'll be all like, "Oh well, maybe..." Irrational self-confidence.

Lesson Thirty-Eight: Money Cannot Be Made

This is something that's going to change the way you view business and money. I want you to understand something. Money cannot be made. I don't even like the saying "making money." We're making money? Nobody's making money. The Federal Reserve makes money. You're not the Federal Reserve. You're an individual. We're not the Rothschilds, we're hustlers, which means we cannot make money. All we can do is take money from other people. Money exists, and we have to take it.

Money's like water, and water is always moving. So you have an ocean, and the sun evaporates the water, it goes into a cloud, and the cloud moves, and then it rains, and then it goes in a river, and it goes to a pond, and then it evaporates again from the sun. Water never stays still. The cycle of precipitation. Some geography for you. And money is like water, it's always moving. And if you stand in the right place at the right time, you're going to get wet. And that's absolutely true. So money cannot be made, it can only be taken from someone else. You stand in the right place at the right time where money's moving, you're going to take it.

99% of people are middlemen. Most people are middlemen. Everyone's a middleman to some degree. Loads of companies exist out there that are just simply middlemen. All they do is... there's something... this is a product, this person wants the product. They're in the middle. They make money. They supply the product. Done. And it really ain't that complicated. They're middlemen.

So money cannot be made. It can only be taken from other people. Every single penny that comes into your bank is not made. It's taken from someone else. Why are they going to give you their money? Why? A serious question. Get a piece of paper and write down, "I have this. I'm selling to this person. They will give me their money because..." and you should be able to name a bunch of reasons. And if you can't, you have a problem.

Don't be thinking about making money. You're not making money, you are taking money. And because you are taking it, you have to convince others to give it to you. That will change the way you approach your marketing, and change the way you view money, change the way you approach your business because that's the reality of what's happening. You're not making it. It's very, very different. You're convincing them, prying it from them.

Lesson Thirty-Nine: Don't Make Anyone Irreplaceable

This is a very simple one, but I've seen it happen time and time again. You're a guy, you're busy, you get an assistant. Your assistant is exceptionally good. Your assistant knows all the passwords, and you don't know, because you're busy, and you're in a rush. You know the end of the story.

Don't make anyone irreplaceable. I wrote this down because I've seen two people lose their companies because they lost either their top salesman or an assistant.

So if your top salesman's floating your company, he's irreplaceable. You need to fix that quickly. So with the agency, we had one salesman who was better than all the rest. He was really, really good, and we didn't make him irreplaceable. And when he left, we really suffered. What I should have done is go to him and say, "You know what, bro? You're really, really good. You're amazing. Do you mind, on Fridays, if every Friday morning you give a speech, or you teach the guys the pitch, or what you're saying on the phone and then you can have Friday afternoon off? I'll give you a day off a week, or I'll give you some extra money, or I'll go out for lunch, or I'll give you a company car. Anything. If you can teach... if you don't mind. You know what, you'd probably do it for free because people like the ego thing, the promotion of telling others what to do. How about every Friday, you can teach the guys, and we can go through the script, and they can learn from you to make the others get up to par, so he's less irreplaceable." Take what he knows.

Never make anybody irreplaceable. If you see or identify someone who's irreplaceable, or you look at your company and go, "I couldn't survive without this person," then you're in trouble. You should always have a company, and you should work with people, it should be fantastic, but you should know that if any of them leave, you can find someone else at all times.

Lesson Forty: Tell People They Can't Have Things

This is another basic sales tactic. You already should know this if you've sold anything before, but you should know, tell people they can't have things all the time. If you tell people they can't have things, they want things. This is the reality of the world.

So let's say someone calls you to buy. Let's say you sell flux capacitors. Let's say you sell flux capacitors, and someone calls up and goes, "I need two flux capacitors, please." The first thing you say to them is, "Oh, yeah, sure, okay, no problem. Let me just check and make sure we have some because they've been in high demand at the moment. I think we might be sold out. I'm not sure we have any. What do you need them for? Oh, I actually want to buy them for XYZ. Okay. I don't... I don't think we have any right now. Let me get back to you. What's your name? Number?"

So what just happened in that exchange? Dude wants the flux capacitor, I am in the middle. In that short exchange, I told him one, he may not be able to have the flux. And two, I asked him why he needs the flux. So one, I told him he can't have it, and two, I asked him why he needs it to reconfirm in his mind that he needs it. "I don't know, we have any. Maybe there's something else. Can I ask what you want to use it for?" "Oh, I need it because..." That's fine. "I don't think we have any."

So he's reconfirmed his need, and I've told him he can't have it. Take away his desire for the flux capacitor. It's higher now than it was before. He wants it more than ever.

So this is obviously one example of how this can be done, but you apply this basic principle: Get them to confirm what they need. Tell them they cannot have it. You cannot have what you want. You cannot have it. You're not allowed it. When I eventually call him back and go, "Okay, how many did you need? Two. Alright, I can get hold of two for you, but it's going to be difficult. Are you looking to purchase right away?" "Oh, well, I'll stick it next week." "Okay, well, I don't know if we're going to even have any then. So bye. Are you going to purchase right away?" "Yeah, I am." If you ask someone, "Are you looking to purchase right away?" and they say yes, it's done. Deal's done.

They're going to mess around, giving you credit card details. They've already said yes. They're looking to purchase right away. Bang! Done! This is sales.

You've managed to fulfill his need. Buy it now. Tell people they cannot have things. Now, a lot of people do this online with the simple, "Running out of time, uh, this book won't be available forever, blah blah blah." But that's because an eBook is available forever. So everyone knows you're just doing it. It's garbage. If you actually could use your brain, think outside the box a little bit. You could find a better way to do it than telling people they can't have things. Telling people they can't have things is a fantastic way to make people want things.

Lesson Forty-One: Why Are You Running Your Business?

This is a genuine question, as a hustler. Why are you running your business? If you don't know the answer, I'll tell you the answer. The answer is for money. That's why you run your business. People will come to you all the time and say, "Start a business you're passionate about." You're only passionate about one thing: cash. It doesn't matter if you sell rocks. It doesn't matter if you sell jellyfish scrotums. Who gives a shit? It doesn't matter what you sell, it matters that it sells. Sell what sells and get rich. Be passionate for profit.

Most people come to me, going, "I need to start a business I know about, and I'm passionate about." No, you don't. I could sell a makeup brand today. I don't know anything about makeup, but I know, with my business acumen, the lessons I've already taught, the way I'd start the company, bringing money in before I put money out, the way that I moved quickly, the way I know I'd make money, I'd make money with a makeup brand. Fact. Fact. And I don't know anything about makeup. Never worn it in my life, ain't got shit to do with it. You don't need to know about things to sell things, you need to know about selling to sell things.

The idea that you need to be passionate about the business to make money from it is complete airy fairy, that idiots say. You are passionate only about what's making you money. You are passionate for profit. You're not passionate about product. So if you can make money selling concrete, let me tell you something. There's some Chinese billionaire out there, who's selling rocks and concrete and making billions. Do you think he's passionate about concrete? Do you think he's making love to concrete, kissing it late at night, hugging it in bed? He doesn't give a fuck about concrete. He gives a fuck about money, as should you. Drop that, "I need to be passionate." Garbage. Passionate for profit only.

Lesson Forty-Two: War is Profitable, But Only If You're Strategic

This is specifically for you, social media marketers. War is profitable, but not always. I get this a lot. I see a lot of people who have digital products constantly in battles with other people in the space, trying to get attention through war, to try and sell products.

War online is very much like real war, and you need to sit and plan and strategize if it's worthwhile. What are your end goals? What are your end objectives? How are you going to achieve them? Is your end goal and objective just to get people paying attention to your tweets? Is your end goal and objective to sell products? Is your end goal and objective to defame and devalue the status of your opponent? What is the end goal and objective?

War can be profitable, but you need to make sure it is worthwhile. You shouldn't be arguing with small accounts, people who are smaller than you. I will only beef with someone if they have more than 10,000 followers. Know your place, know their place.

War can be profitable, but you need a strategy for war. So I had a clear objective for my battle. Most people will go viral, or they'll go into battle, and they haven't got a clear objective. They don't know what they're trying to do.

So if you're going to go to war, in any way, either in the physical world or the internet reality, you need to be prepared, and you're not prepared without a strategy. So war is only profitable if you have a strategy, have a clear end goal, have a clear objective. Don't end up like America, stuck in the Middle East in a forever, endless, pointless, nothing war. That's what most people online are doing, constantly jabbing at each other for no reason. It's pathetic.

I don't go to war often, and if I go to war, it's going to pay me. I don't lose money to go to war. War is profitable, but only if you do it right. Keep that in mind.

Lesson Forty-Three: FOMO Sells

This is something you already know. You're thinking, "hey, I already know that." How do you instill FOMO? Well, here's how.

Most of you guys instill FOMO by saying, "If you don't buy now, we're closing, and you won't be able to buy." No one cares because we know that's a lie. And we know that you're just closing it artificially to try and make some artificial deadline. So no one cares.

How do I instill FOMO? I talk about how many other people have already bought it. "All these people over here know what I know. You don't know." Talk about other people buying your product, and it will make people want to buy your product because they'll feel like they missed out.

So with advertising, I do this all the time. I constantly talk about other campaigns or other clients I had, not in a braggy way, just in a... when I'm doing business with this, or I did this campaign for this data, or this is actually a very busy time of year for us right now.

If 15 people signed up in the last two weeks, we're really busy. Lots of people are doing this. Everyone's involved. People are doing this, people are doing this, people are doing this. "Oh, I don't want to miss out. Everyone else is doing it." Maybe everyone else does have a good idea. Why do I think it's a good idea? Well, I don't like this, and I don't like that, but everyone else likes it. So okay...

Even very successful people are sheep. If they think everyone else is doing it, they're going to do it. It's the same with fashion trends. How many stupid, dumb pieces of clothing have you seen people wearing? Everyone else is wearing it. People need to know that lots of other people are buying. You need to find a way to make that clear. "Lots of people are buying. Lots of people are doing this. You're the one who's not doing it."

So with this book, I told the truth. I've been very, very impressed with how many signups I've had. I've not lied. I didn't need to because I've had lots of signups. But lots of people are learning all of my secrets to making money. You don't know that, but that person has FOMO now. I don't need to say I'm closing the book. I need to say, "Look, these guys know a whole bunch of stuff you don't know." I did this all the time with advertising. It was fantastic with advertising. "This is a really busy time of year for us." I used to say this. You know what, any time of year: January, February, March, April, May, June, July, August, September, October, November, didn't matter. Do you know what I'd say? I'd say, "This is a really busy time of year for us because people are gearing up for Christmas." They're like, "Christmas? It's March!" I'm like, "Yeah, exactly. People are preparing already for the Christmas rush. It's March. So now they're sitting there going, 'It's March, we haven't even thought about Christmas yet.' All these other businesses are thinking about Christmas. They're thinking about doing adverts at Christmas. It's March. We haven't even thought about Christmas." "Yeah, yeah. Oh, yo, oh, Christmas."

I used to say that any time of year, December 1st or January 1st. I'd say, January 1st, I used to say when I go to meetings and say, "You know what's funny about January?" To say what? I'd say, "We sign up most of our Christmas advertising this month." They go, "Really?" "Oh, yeah, yeah. We're preparing for Christmas in January."

After Christmas, everyone's made a lot of money with advertising. People have made a lot of money in the campaigns we've already run, so now they're already preparing for the next campaigns at Christmas. So we're actually gearing up for Christmas right now. People be sitting there going, "Oh, maybe I need to do a campaign for Christmas." Other people are doing things, you're not doing anything. You are lazy, you are slow. Other people are ahead of you. Quickly get on the train. The train's leaving. Quickly get on, quickly pay the invoice. That's how you do it. I do it all the time with advertising. Talk about other people buying it, it sells. Always talk about other people buying. Super important, because it sells.

Instills some confidence in them that you're a real person, a real company.

It allows their thinking to be checked. "Well, I think it's a good idea, and all these other people think it's a good idea, so...let me try to"

I have something called social proof. I pay money to have that thing at the bottom that tells people every time someone buys my website. So when you go on my website, you see other people are learning. You're not learning, but other people are. FOMO.

Lesson fourty-Four: Chaos and Opportunity

I once got told that chaos and opportunity are the same word in Japanese. I don't know if that's true, but I'm going to say it. Chaos and opportunity are the same word in Japanese.

In other words, every cloud has a silver lining. Every time stuff's fucked up, every time there's chaos, every time there's a mess, there is an opportunity, a huge opportunity, and you have to find a way to identify it one way or another. That's all it is. There's always a way to identify it. So what's the chaos? What's the fuck-up? I don't know, off the top of my head. It doesn't matter what it is. The point is, you already applied speed to fix it, but you need to find a way to twist it in your favor. There's always a way to twist it in your favor.

So it doesn't matter what it is. Let's say your backend isn't done properly. Your backend is missing a bunch of vital information. Let's say, okay, cool, so you need a whole bunch of orders. You need something.

You need people to fill in some information to fill in the backend. Then you hit up all your customers with a ridiculous deal: 99 cents for our face screen, usually $10.99. 99 cents if you buy with any other product. Some ridiculous deal, even if it's a break-even. What do you get? You get a whole bunch of orders. It fills in your backend. Your backend's back. Even if you just broke even on it, you filled in your backend. You've got some more loyal customers who are more prepared, and more used to spending money on your website. Bang! Done.

There's always an opportunity. It doesn't matter how fucked up things go wrong. There's always an opportunity somewhere. You just need to find it. Sniff it out. Something's gone wrong. There must be some way here I can make some money. And everything has to feedback to, remember, the money in. That's important.

Chaos and opportunity are the same thing. Especially, that's chaos within your business. There's chaos within your market, it's even better. So I don't know. Let's say, okay, let's talk about 9/11. That fucked up the airline industry. All the planes got grounded. No one could fly. Huge lines at the airports, chaos. There's chaos within the industry. So where's the opportunity? This is off the top of my head. If I was an airline executive, boss, I'd be going, "Okay, from now on when we sell tickets, we're going to sell it with an added option for insurance for refunds, in the event of a terror attack or an unpredictable event. We're going to contact a big insurance company, where to get them to insure us. We don't have to really do anything. We get them to insure us, and we'll sell the insurance packages on top at a premium, and make some extra money. Because now people are... who've been stuck in the airport for four days. Next time they book a flight, they're going to be like, 'Yeah, you know what? I'm going to pay for that insurance.' Remember last time? It was a nightmare. If I pay for this, I get all my money back, and they'll book me a hotel." Bang! Chaos in the industry, opportunity to make more money.

This came to me off the top of my head. Where else was there huge chaos in an industry? Can you think of chaos in an industry? It happens now and again. Now and again, things really go wrong. So no, but it happens all the time on smaller levels. And when there's chaos within a specialized industry, you need to find a way to monetize it, like I just did there with 9/11 and the airlines. Because there's always a way to monetize chaos.

So when things go wrong, it happens. So like, the YouTube apocalypse, for example, everything went super, super wrong with all the YouTubers who were making loads and loads of money off advertising, and then the apocalypse happened. They weren't making money off advertising anymore. So let's say that I'm a YouTuber, and I see this happen. There's huge chaos in the industry. No one's making money off advertising anymore. Do you know what you do? Well, I'd go, "Okay, well, that means I need to sell merchandise." So I'd contact all the other big YouTubers and say, "Hey, I've got a really good link for merchandise. If you're interested in selling merch..." I start a merch company, or I get a link with a merch company for commission. It's not complicated.

So let's look at the adpocalypse. Everyone, I don't know if you know what happened, everyone had all these big YouTube channels, they're making loads and loads and loads of money, overnight, that all goes down to zero. Now they've still got viewership, but they've got no money. So how do they make money from there? Well, they all decide to start selling merchandise, but they don't have any merchandise set up for them, or worked out. Me, as a big YouTuber, I contact a merchandise company, explain the adpocalypse, explain what happened, explain I want to produce my own merchandise, and explain that I know 10 other big YouTubers who are going to go to another merchandise company, but I'm going to bring them to you if you'll give me a cut of how much money they bring you. And they'll... anyone in their right mind would go, "Well, okay, get on the phone." Old school. Yeah, I know 10 other YouTubers who I've met with and I work with, blah, blah. They were going to use this merch website, school another one, and I'm saying, "I want to use you, but if I bring them all to you, I want five percent of their turnover." They'll agree. Bang! Now, from the chaos in the industry, you've become the fucking shark of merch. Now you're making money off all of their YouTube channels with one phone call by just being a GENIUS AND WITH SPEED. Before, you didn't get none of their money, you just knew them. Now all you have to do is call them up and say,"Bro adpocalypse is, but I know an awesome company that's going to sell us merch. We're going to sell merch and make money." Bang! Chaos in the industry is an opportunity, every time.

If you think like me, if you think like a hustler, this is setting up a company, a revenue stream, it costs you nothing. There's no outlay to this. This is just a phone call and a hustler's mindset. Bang, you got paid. Chaos is opportunity. Find it every time.

Lesson Forty-Five: View Your Offers from Your Buyer's Eyes

This is super important. You have to learn to view all of your offers from your buyer's eyes. You have to understand why that's so important. The Federal Reserve can make money. They can print money. You can't. There's only one way you're going to make money. I'm going to give you a demonstration of how that happens.

This is Mr. Customer. This is his money. This is you. He gives it to you. Beautiful. Very complicated, I know. That is how you make money. You don't print money, you don't generate money. You make money because people decide to give it to you. So you have to learn how to view your offer very, very specifically from your buyer's eyes. This is point number 45.

So your offer is whatever... "I am the best surgeon, masseuse, who the fuck knows, blah blah blah." You have to... you're thinking about it from your point of view. Oh, I see this all the time with people.

"Oh, but people are going to come do business with us because our oil is the best, our massage oil is the best." Does he know anything about massage oil? Does he even give a shit? Has he tried bad massage oil? Does he know the difference? Has he felt the difference between good and bad massage oil? Like, you think... I see this all the time with people. They think nitpicking, tiny little details is going to make the money.

I took massage completely at random, but let's use it as an example. You have a massage company, that's supposed to say massage. You think, "Oh, we use the best massage oil, that's why we're the most expensive, and people are going to come to us." If you actually, instead of being like most people who run their businesses, you're a geek, you're a massage oil geek. It doesn't matter if you're a programmer geek, or a mechanic geek, or whatever your business is, a dropshipping geek, anything, it doesn't matter. You would understand that from the buyer's perspective, they don't give a shit about massage oil. They don't know the difference in different kinds of massage oil, and they don't even know how... they don't even know the benefit of using a good massage oil.

They've never used a bad massage oil. They don't know how bad a bad massage oil is for them. Oil is oil.

So you're not viewing the product... you're not viewing the offer from the eyes of the consumer. You're reviewing the offer from the eyes of you, a knowledgeable nerd. Most consumers are not knowledgeable, especially on what you're trying to sell them. They don't know anything. You have to view it from their eyes. If you rooted from their eyes, you'd understand they don't give a shit about massage oil.

So then your choices are as follows: Either you educate them on massage oil. You incorporate that into your advertising, and teach them and explain to them why it's better, or you fuck it off and get something cheaper, and save money. Those are the two genuine options.

Always look from your buyer's eyes. Why is your buyer going to give you money and do this? Intricately, like, do it down to the tiny details. It doesn't matter. We'll go back to a coffee shop. Why are they going to come get coffee with me? Because my chairs are comfortable? Because my building looks warm? I use the same lights we have in here,

Edison bulbs, to make it look warm. My staff, I've got a couple of cute girls there. My cups are cool, I got colored cups. It doesn't matter. You need to think of everything. Why would someone walk past my coffee shop and go, "Yeah, I actually do want coffee?"

You have to think about it at that level for every single product you sell. Why you and not someone else? Because there's always someone else selling. So you're viewing yourself from the buyer's eyes. While you're doing that, you can view your competition from the buyer's eyes. So if you do, in this example, this is the competition, he uses cheap massage oil, but he's cheaper than you. So from the buyer's eyes, he's like, "Okay, masseuse, masseuse. He's 20 bucks cheaper. Massage is a massage. I'll just go with him." They'll go with the cheap guy first. And unless it's absolutely awful, they're not going to upgrade. Now, I've said many times, "Don't sell on price." So I'm not saying you should try to out-pressure your competition. My point is, if he is viewing the two of you, and the only difference he can identify is the cost, why would he buy the most expensive one? So you need to understand here, "Okay, my job here is to identify my USP, which is the expensive massage oil, and educate my consumers as to why they should use it."

So every time someone calls you, on any poster, anything like that, you need to be saying, "Guaranteed, no skin irritation, or guaranteed best results for acne." Whatever, anything that can make people go, "Why is that guaranteed? What..." And you can explain to them, "Oh, we actually use this kind of oil, other people use cheap oil from China. We don't use that. We use oil which is hand-pressed in the Italian mountains." Blah blah blah blah. View yourself from your buyer's eyes, otherwise, you end up not selling it. Think about that seriously. You can do this on so many levels. It doesn't matter what product you have, it doesn't matter what you're selling, view yourself from the buyer. Identify why they're going to do business with you above someone else, and never assume the buyer has knowledge.

This happens all the time where people go, "Oh, but actually my company does this, and my company does that." And my comment is, "Yeah, but no one knows that, and no one cares." You think that matters? It doesn't matter. You think that matters? It doesn't matter at all.

You need to educate the buyer. While that matters, otherwise, you don't give a SHIT. view yourself in the buyer's eyes. Do not view yourself from your own knowledgeable eyes.

Lesson Forty-Six: Ask Your Mom About Your Company

This feeds perfectly into the last lesson. If you want an unbiased opinion from a general consumer on your company, I'll tell you who you get it from. Number 46: Ask your mother about your company. It doesn't matter what company you want to launch, go and ask your mother about it.

I'll tell you why. Your mother is very INNOCENT, she's going to be very indicative of a typical consumer. She isn't going to know a lot about what you're trying to do. She isn't going to know a lot about technical stuff. She isn't really going to understand a lot of the things you say.

If you have an idea for a company, you're a masseuse, and you go to your mom, "Hey, I'm going to open a massage company."

"Really? You're not a massage company. Why? Why?"

"I think I can make money making massages."

"Well, how much is it going to cost? This much? That's expensive for a massage."

If that's the first thing she says, you've got a problem.

"No, it's not expensive because we use the best massage oil."

"Well, what's the difference in massage oil? It's all the same, isn't it?"

Bang! Your mother is going to give you the best market research you're ever going to have in your life. Now, if you're selling something super specialized, and your mom may not understand, then maybe, I don't know, a little bit more difficult. But for anything basically normal, you should ask your mom about your company because she's going to identify all your problems straight away. That conversation I just had, imaginary conversation I had with my mom, she identified that I'm coming across as expensive and that no one gives a shit about massage oil. Bang! There's your problem identified.

Your mom's never going to lie to you. She's always going to be straight to the point and explain to you exactly what your issues are and what needs to be solved. Any company you're launching, you need to show to and speak to your mom about because she's going to cut the bullshit faster than anyone.

Please, remember: Your average, typical consumer is

not an educated person. Because most average people in the world aren't educated people. They don't have much knowledge of anything, and they certainly don't have knowledge of your particular subject. And they don't have specialist knowledge of your subject.

I don't know about you. I mean, I'm a professional karate player. I've been getting massages where I've been training hard for many, many years. When I walk into a massage parlor, and they say, "Do you want a sports massage? A Swedish massage? This massage? That massage?" I don't... I still don't know the difference. I don't know. They're all the same, aren't they? I don't know. "Oh, I just go, 'Oh, okay, this one.'" So I don't even know about massages, and I've probably had more massages than most people. And this is my point exactly: Your consumer is not educated, so... and you need to educate them, and make them understand why you're charging more, or you need to remove that barrier.

So when I just gave that conversation with the mom there, with the massage oil, she's already identified it as expensive. She's identified, "No one gives a fuck about massage oil." Your mom is going to tell you what ideas are good and what aren't, and she's never,

ever going to lie to you. But you know why? Because your mother wants you to be successful. Your mother does not want you wasting your time on some company that's never going to pay you. Your mother wants you to do well. So any idea you have, go to your mom, and say, "Dude, what do you think of this company?" See what she says. And then if she sits there and she says, "Only good thing, say, 'What would you buy from me?' 'No, cause I don't want that.' 'Why don't you want it?' 'Well, I don't know.'" Don't start writing down all the reasons she wouldn't buy from you. Why doesn't she want it? Why wouldn't she buy from you? Work out how to overcome all of these things.

You're going to get a whole bunch of information. So you're speaking to your mom, ask her, have a general conversation about the company, and then ask her why she would or wouldn't buy from you, and make sure you write that information down.

She says, "I would buy from you because XYZ." Good. Those are your points you need to press home in all your advertising.

So she wouldn't buy from you because XYZ. You need to go, "Okay, how do I solve this?

How do I overcome these? Why wouldn't you buy a massage from me, Mom? 'I don't have time.' Oh, we have mobile masseuses, though. We come around. We'll come to your house if you haven't got time. 'Oh, yeah, but you know, uh...' 'Well, how do I book it?' 'We'll put a flyer through your door and you can just book by text message.' Okay." Like anything to overcome, find out what her problems are, and overcome them.

So you have to speak to your mom about every single company. This is super important because it's the best market research you're going to get. If you can do your market research in advance, before you launch your company, that's less time you're going to spend fucking up, more time you're going to spend making money.

So every single company... I bought my new Lamborghini, and I drove to my mom's house. I said, "Mom, what do you think of my new car?" She goes, "What is that?" It says Lamborghini. She goes, "How much was it?" I said, "It was $300 grand." She goes, "Three? You spent $300 grand on a car?" It's like, "Yeah." She goes, "Let me see."

So she comes out, and she says something that was so

stupid, it circled back around to smart. She looked at my Lamborghini, and she goes, "Why would you spend $300,000 on something that only has two seats? It should have more seats because it costs more money. So I should have got a bus for my money." I guess that's her logic. Her logic is, "Why would you? It's only got two seats." So which is stupid, but it kind of gets into the smart realm. It's kind of, you know, you get a lot of these kinds of comments from mothers. They say things which are kind of dumb, but kind of smart, and you can extract those comments and apply them to your company. You'll fix a lot of problems in advance. So that's why speaking to your mom is so important.

Lesson Forty-Seven: Money Will Never Motivate Your Staff

This is very, very important. I'm going to tell you a story with this one. Money will never motivate your staff. Never. And I'll tell you why.

Money is numbers, and numbers never end. Which means if you're going to try to motivate people with money, it's going to get hard. If someone doesn't like the job, and doesn't like you, and doesn't like anything about how they're treated in the job, or how they feel, or what they do, you have to pay them a lot of money to make them do it. A lot of money, and that is not very, very cost-effective.

If somebody enjoys what they do, and they feel part of a community, and they like it, then you don't pay much at all.

Remember, after my first business, I started an agency, my own company to sell advertising. So what happened is I found an office in my town that was £400 a month, and I decided I was going to become a millionaire advertising. So I found a £400 office. Me and my brother would sit there. And then we advertised for salesmen, commission only. So it was a commission-only position. You sent emails all day long. Just emailing marketing managers all day. All day. Just copy and pasting, just emailing anyone you could find on the internet, emailing all day long. If they replied to you, there'd be a phone call. I'd do the phone call. So the company was all phone pitching. And that's why it took a long time for us to train our staff. Every single day, we were doing two hours of training: phone pitching about advertising, phone pitching, phone pitching, phone pitching.

 The company made money, but training people to be good on the phones is hard, and a lot of people are scared to do cold calls. Well, and people are lazy with cold calls. So I'm interested, the idea, you know what? "We're going to email blast anyone we can find. We'll buy all the magazines, email every marketing manager. We'll go through all of the websites we can find." We'd Google up things like "store locator." If you type "store locator" into Google, you have all the companies that have store locators. These are companies with multiple branches. So advertising will suit them because it's... they're across their national... the national... email, email, email. If any marketing manager emailed back, I'd do the call because I'm trained on the phone. So the company was... everyone pitched on their own. It's just emails out. So we put adverts out there for a position which was commission only, so no basic... every deal you landed you got five percent. So if you landed a £20,000 deal on websites and other media, you'd get a thousand pounds. So if you landed two a month, you'd get two grand a month. Ain't going to make you rich, but whatever. And we were hiring basically anyone. Like it doesn't matter. Like we had one guy who had a criminal record. We had one dude who's just a bit of a weirdo. Some fat guy with... some other guy who definitely drank too much, because he stunk of booze. But who cares? They're coming in, they're sending the emails. And then someone emailed back. I'd call them.

Over time, as people came and quit, and didn't land any deals, we ended up with a good little team of four guys, plus me and my brother. So six guys who are in this office now. These guys were working hard. They were emailing like machines, because you can't get machine to email, because you've got to go to the websites, find their email marketing manager's name. You can buy email marketing manager lists, but they never worked because it changes so often. This... so we had to go and manually find and manually type it in. So these guys are emailing, emailing, my email, emailing, anyway.

Most of the guys I had there for the first solid month didn't make a penny. I had free staff for a month. I had four guys supposed to be interested, and they're working their asses off for free. How did I motivate them? Every day, I'd come in, positive energy. Come in full of energy. "Guys, today's... today we're going to make it! Oh, your guy emailed back! I'm calling him later. That's a deal. That's definitely able to do this. A long time, it might take a few weeks. That's going to be a deal." And I'd order pizza every day. I'd order pizza. We'd sit around. We'd eat our pizza in the office. I'd talk about the big dreams of how our first agency was such a big company, how the company is going to be bigger. I'd sell a dream. And they'd eat pizza. And everything was fine.

So for a $10 pizza every day, I had four members of full-time staff. Now, none of these men were motivated by my energy, the dreams of the future. They weren't getting paid anything. They may have been motivated by the future prospect of money, but I hadn't offered them any money to turn up, and they were on time every single day.

You do not need money to motivate your staff. If your staff respect you, and they know where you're going, and things are going to go well, then you don't need money to motivate them.

I actually fucked up big here because what happened with this company is I accepted a fight. And I decided to go training in Slovakia. When I went away for 10 days, in the 10 days in the office, all the men quit. Every single one. And that was the end of my company. The whole business fell apart. And that's because we weren't there. The leaders had abandoned ship. They felt there's no leadership energy in the office. There's no one buying pizza. "Why am I coming here every day for free?" All of a sudden, it dawns on them, and they leave.

But the point I'm trying to make with this story is number 47 is that money will never motivate your staff. There are better ways to motivate your staff. Obviously, pay your staff well. Obviously, they need money, give them money. I'm not saying you can get them all to work for free. My point is, I see loads of people who go, "I'll start a company and I'm going to pay my guys the most." And I saw this with a fight promotion. So there's a fight promotion that comes along, goes, "I'm gonna launch the biggest fight promotion. Some guys I know with money, big buddy as well, we want to launch a kickboxing promotion." "So how you gonna be the biggest?" "We're going to pay all the fighters the biggest money, the most money, so they all want to fight for us. Get the best fighters." Sounds like a good idea, especially for fighters because most fighters are broke. The problem is, they didn't end up getting the best fighters because they didn't have good exposure. They didn't have good cameras, they didn't... have good social media platforms. So a lot of fighters were choosing to fight other places because of the prestige they got for winning, as opposed to this organization, not even heard of. And a couple extra hundred bucks doesn't motivate.

There are far better ways to motivate than money in life. So don't be thinking you need to pay your staff loads of money to make them loyal to you. That's complete shit, that's not true at all. Get that in your head. Money doesn't motivate.

Lesson Forty-Eight: Success Is Exponential

This is something I've already been discussing at length, but it's so important, we're going to go over it again. When you've done something once, it's much quicker to do it again. It's the same with anything. You'll say, you start driving, you parallel park once, it takes forever. Eventually, you get a parallel parking, it's quick. It's exactly the same with success. Success is exponential. As you've done things, it becomes quicker to do things.

It takes a long time to make a million. It's easier to make a second million. It's even easier to make a third. It's easier to make a fourth, because you understand the mechanisms.

So starting from the very, very bottom, if you can stay motivated and work hard when you have nothing, you're in the hardest part. It does get easier. The problems change as you get bigger and become a bigger company. You may have legal problems, or fulfillment issues, or all these other problems, but you won't be broke anymore, at least.

I believe business gets easier. It starts hard, H for hard, and gets easier. If you can stick it out here, you'll enjoy MOST IN FUTURE. Most people quit here. 99% of people quit when it's hard, and that's why the one percent is the one percent. It's exponential.

The first time you make a website, you have to go out there. You have to source all these different companies. You have to find a member of staff to make it. And you make it, and you make mistakes, and you need to change it because the SEO ain't set up, blah blah, whatever. The third, fourth, fifth, sixth, seventh time you make a website, you can do it very, very quickly. You can do it properly the first time, without mistakes.

So success is exponential. Keep that in mind. That anything that seems to be taking forever now, remember lesson one: speed, speed, speed, speed, speed. We're going to get better. You're going to get faster at it, and soon, things are going to blow up quickly.

I launch companies every day. I can launch a company, I can launch a new company a day. I've got to that point now. I know my people, my staff are good. I can say, "James, do this. Dylan, do this. Luke, do this. BRO do this. You do this, you do that, you do this, I'll do this." Bang! And within six hours, everything's done. I'm at that point now. But that's come from so much success previously. It's exponential. It builds up. So keep that in mind now.

Lesson Forty-Nine: nobody is broke.

They're simply just buying other stuff. They're buying other things. People go, "I can't afford it." That means, "Well, I can afford it, but I decided I need something else more." Broke people are not broke, they just want something else more than they want your offer. Your offer has to be more important than food.

So what you offer, whatever it is... what are we selling, flux capacitors? No matter what it is, it has to be more important than food, because when broke people say they can't afford it, unless they're literally poor on the street, which is quite rare, they're still buying food, and they're probably still buying, paying for their car, paying for their rent. They're going out on the weekend with their friends. They're still socializing. They're still paying for that ski trip next month. So they're paying for plenty of stuff. They're just not paying for what you've got. So no one's broke. They just decide that other things are more important than what you offer.

So how do you get around that? Well, you have to make sure your offer is always geared as more important. Some of you guys who bought this, literally, it was all your money, but you thought, "I need this. I don't need to go out in the club. I need this book instead." So I convinced you, and you made the right decision. I didn't convince you in a negative way. I convinced you in a correct way because you made a very smart decision. But I convinced you that my knowledge and this course are more important than going to the club, or eating at an expensive restaurant, or some dumb shit. I convinced you of that.

So nobody is broke, they're just buying other things. Get out of your head the idea that people can't afford things. They can't afford it, they just don't want it enough. Because if they wanted it, they'd buy it. Because they're buying a whole bunch of other things. Everyone is spending money every day. They're buying other things. So how do you convince people your offer is worth more than something as basic as food?

Well, that's very, very simple. You just promise it's going to lead to more food later. Done.

So, and that's the truth with houses, university, so why is this book worth more than anything else you could do? Because if you listen to the advice in here, and start your own business, you can do that on later. More! It's exactly the point. So let's say you still sell flux capacitors, and you say to somebody, "Buy one." "I can't afford it." "Yeah, you can." "No, I can't. I can't, I've got to pay my rent. Blah blah blah blah." "Say, well, if you buy a flux capacitor, your rent's going to reduce. So in the long run, you're not going to pay as much rent. For example, or if you buy a flux capacitor, you're going to have more food. Or you're going to make more money, so you can buy more food. Or you're going to have your own farm. Who gives a... what? Find a way to get around people's objections, so that they understand that buying your product is more important than doing any of the other dumb things they do.

Nobody is poor. Everybody's a customer, and everybody has some money. You have to get around it. So let's say you're selling gas and oil supplies. I don't know anything about gas and oil supplies. I also don't know how you sell it. I don't know your particular selling tactic, however, I'm sure you make it very, very clear to people when you try to sell them a new pipe, "You need this new pipe. You need this new pipe. I can't afford it." "But if you buy this new pipe, you're going to save money. You can't afford to not have it because you're going to save money if you buy it. So if your problem is money, then you really need this pipe." Bang! Flipped on them. "Your problem's money? You told me you have no money, well, now you need the pipe, otherwise, you're going to never have money." Now the pipe's more important to saving money. Go buy the pipe.

You have to make everyone understand that your offer is more important than anything else they can possibly buy. If they put something else above it... more important, like food, air, water, promise them more food, air, and water if they buy your product. Nobody is broke, they just need to want it. And you have to make people want it. That is your goal. So get out your idea. Alright?

Now, here, all the time, from business owners,"Oh, it's a slow period right now." Why? "Oh, the recession, or people ain't got much money right now." Complete garbage! Complete... people are broke? It's completely untrue. You just have to make your offer more appealing than anything else they can possibly spend their money on, and they'll buy your offer. And you do that by either promising more of something else, or positioning yourself above something else. Very, very easy.

Lesson Fifty: You're Lazy

This is a point that's been deliberately chosen to be point fifty so I can tell you something that you already know about yourselves. Halfway through this BOOK, you already know what to do for your business. You already know how to make money. You're lazy.

 I'll give you an example. The other day, I was talking to some girl in my life. She's talking, obviously, about how she wants to run a makeup company. I said, "If you want to run a makeup company, why don't you have a makeup company?" She goes, "Oh, yeah, I know, but you know, I don't know what to do." I said, "Okay, I'll tell you exactly what to do. Here's what you do: Go to alibaba.com. Get some samples of makeup. Find one you like. Put a new sticker on it. Make a website. Sell on your website. Get YouTubers who talk about makeup to talk about your makeup brand. Sell makeup. Done. You're in a makeup company." She goes, "That's a good idea, actually." I go, "Yeah, it is." A week later, I said, "How much makeup you sold?" "What do you mean? It's like, I told you how to do an entire makeup brand from start to finish, so you do an entire company. How much have you sold?" It was all well, she did nothing. Seven days, she did nothing.

I told her how to run a whole company. You wanted to run a makeup brand, I just told you how to do it. Didn't do it.

Although you are out there already sitting on ideas, guess why you're not doing them? Because you're lazy. You know how to do it, but you won't do it. You already know what you should do. You already know how to do it, but you're not doing it because you're lazy. You already have the idea, go, stop waiting. Number one, speed is everything. What are you waiting for? If you would have started the idea a week ago, it'd be ready by now.

You're around a lot of people out there with business ideas, they already know what to do, they just are lazy, and they don't get it done. If you're waiting, hoping you need some kind of investment, or you're waiting for something, you should have learned enough in the first half of this book that you don't need investment. You can get the money coming in without investment. We've already discussed that. There is nothing to wait for.

I hear all the time, man, people don't realize how often they do it. I hear people say, "Oh, I've got this idea for a business." "Let's say, cool. A month later, yeah, I'm working on my idea." A month? Do you have any idea what I could achieve in a month? A month? I have an idea, it's ready, same day.

You know what to do. You're all slow, and you're all lazy. That's the reality. That's point fifty. You need to accept that about yourself and accept that if you really had the tenacity that you desire, if you really have the tenacity to get what you desire, if you're really like me, a go-getter, a warrior, you'd already be doing too much waiting, too much talking, not enough action.

www.ingramcontent.com/pod-product-compliance
Lightning Source LLC
Chambersburg PA
CBHW071052240526
45471CB00015B/1646